Remembering Dad

Remembering Dad

Gary Vermeer's Daughter Recalls His Life and Legacy

Mary Andringa

ISBN: 978-0-9983058-8-2

Published and printed in the United States of America by
the Write Place, Inc. For more information, please contact:

the Write Place, Inc.
809 W. 8th Street, Suite 2
Pella, Iowa 50219
www.thewriteplace.biz

Cover and interior design by Michelle Stam, the Write Place, Inc.
Paper stock image by piart, thinkstock.com.
Photo corner stock image by FreeTransform, thinkstock.com.

Copies of this book may be ordered online at Amazon and
BarnesandNoble.com.

View other Write Place titles at www.thewriteplace.biz.

Table of Contents

Preface... i
Acknowledgments iii

1. Roots...1
2. Equality...23
3. Skeptical and Curious....................................39
4. Heart of an Entrepreneur 57
5. Communication..73
6. Tools for Success 85
7. Practical Leadership.....................................103
8. Lean Processes 129
9. Philanthropy 159
10. Enhancing Community 177

Source Notes 201

Preface

"How did your Dad start Vermeer Corporation? How did he grow the company?" These are questions Vermeer customers have asked me many times. My nieces and nephews have also asked me about their grandfather's philosophy on a variety of topics.

These questions, and the upcoming one-hundredth anniversary of Dad's birth, have motivated me to write about my father and what I learned from him. Even though he is no longer among us, I continue to realize in many situations how much I learned just by seeing and imitating his model.

While doing research for this book, I became fascinated by stories others have told me that have provided new information and insight into Dad's life. He truly was—as he once said himself—more complicated than most people think.

Through this book about Dad, I want his grandchildren and future generations of his descendants to know more of his stories. A study by Emory University reveals the importance of passing on a legacy:

> *Children who know stories about relatives who came before them show higher levels of emotional well-being, according to Emory University researchers who analyzed dinnertime conversations and other measures of how well families work... Family stories provide a sense of identity through time, and help children understand who they are in the world.*[1]

In the course of my research about Dad, I discovered interesting historical tidbits that were not about him. I opted to include some of these stories as sidebars. Some of them were just too good to pass up!

The chapters which follow are not, of course, a comprehensive story of my father's life. I'm sure my brothers, Bob and Stan, could write their own books of memories. What I have recorded are my memories and the memories of the people I interviewed.

As I was putting the final touches on the manuscript, new items kept popping up. For example, just recently I stumbled across multiple references to Dad laughing so hard about a good story that tears began rolling down his cheeks, and I realized I hadn't mentioned that. He certainly loved a good belly laugh!

I know, though, that a book can never do justice to a life, and it is time to declare this manuscript complete. Vermeer Corporation will celebrate its seventieth anniversary in 2018, along with the twentieth anniversary of our Lean or Continuous Improvement Journey. And 2018 marks the one-hundredth anniversary of my father's birth.

Could there be a better time to share my memories, both with those who knew him and those who did not?

Happy one-hundredth birthday, Dad!

Acknowledgments

I am not able to name everyone who contributed their thoughts, stories, and perceptions about Dad to this book, but I am grateful to each one and I do want to mention a few by name.

My brothers, Stan and Bob, were both very helpful in sharing their memories of certain historical events in our lives. Since I am seven years younger than Stan and five years younger than Bob, my perspective and interactions with Dad were somewhat different than theirs. I also believe there is a special relationship between a father and daughter.

My uncle, John Vermeer, the third son in my dad's family, recently passed away at the age of ninety-two. He was my second dad since I lived with Uncle John and Aunt Effie during a couple of the long trips my parents took while I was in junior high and high school. As I was writing this book, Uncle John was a fantastic contributor of stories about growing up on the farm, family connections to the Michigan relatives, and fishing and hunting incidents. It was a pleasure for me to visit him several times a month over the last couple years. Often when I went to visit, he had a new story for me.

The staff at the Vermeer archives, Gloria Van Wyk and Candy Van Zante, have been wonderful in searching through the archives for historical documents and pictures that relate to some of the stories in this book. Gloria in particular took on her role of searching for information very enthusiastically. She has served the company in various capacities for over fifty years. She served as my assistant for a number of years, but she was also one of the employees who knew Dad well and shared her own stories of Gary at work and in Canada.

I am grateful to a number of key Vermeer and dealership employees who were generous with their time in sharing the stories they remember about Dad. Other friends of my parents in Pella and outside Pella were also so helpful and shared their stories with me.

I am extremely thankful for the wonderful editor I have found in Carol Van Klompenburg. As co-author of the 2008 book *In Search of a Better Way*, which is about my parents' lives, she knew Dad. She had interviewed my parents a dozen times before writing the book, so her understanding of the personalities of my parents and her knowledge of many of the stories was extremely helpful.

Our children, Jason and Mindi, have also contributed their stories of their grandfather. I not only appreciate their reflections on their grandfather, but also their loving respect and admiration for him. They have been supportive during this project, just as they were during the years when they were growing up and were flexible as I balanced parenting and my roles at Vermeer.

Most importantly, I want to acknowledge my husband, Dale, who read many of my first drafts, joined in several interviews, and suggested additional stories or encouraged me to elaborate on them. Dale is known as a storyteller who loves to add extra color to stories. He provided me with details—most of which I believe are true! Dale has not only supported me in this project, he has also been a fantastic partner in life for over forty-five years.

1 | Roots

The Impact of Earlier Generations

As a child, I adored my father. It was a generational pattern, I think, because Dad had adored his own father, Jacob Vermeer. Whenever Dad talked to me about Grandpa Jacob, he spoke with great love and respect.

IN HIS FATHER'S FOOTSTEPS

Growing up, Dad worked alongside his father on the farm. He learned how to tile the water from a field for better agricultural use of the land. He learned how to use horses to do the farm work. He also observed how his father put his law diploma from Chicago Correspondence School of Law to practical use, writing wills, deeds of sale, and other contracts for families, friends, and acquaintances.

We still have Jacob's law books from 1915, with his notes and letters inserted between pages. One letter, entitled "CROP REPORT—SPECIAL," is addressed to Jacob G. Ver Meer and dated January 19, 1931. The letter was sent from the Department of Agriculture in Des Moines and contained livestock estimates for Iowa and the surrounding states. As a good farmer, Jacob used available sources of information to help him farm wisely.

Dad also observed his father's extensive work in the local community. Jacob served on boards for First Christian Reformed Church of Pella, the Pella Farmers' Coop, the Pella

National Bank, and Plainview Country School. When Jacob attended Plainview school, it was located one mile east of Pella, on the corner of what is now Vermeer Corporation head-

UNITED STATES DEPARTMENT OF AGRICULTURE
BUREAU OF AGRICULTURAL ECONOMICS
DIVISION OF CROP AND LIVESTOCK ESTIMATES
DES MOINES, IOWA.

January 17, 1931.

CATTLE ON FEED JANUARY 1, 1931.

The number of cattle on feed for market in the eleven Corn Belt States was 10 per cent smaller on January 1, 1931 than on January 1, 1930 according to the cattle feeding estimate of the Department of Agriculture. In the 5 states east of the Mississippi River the decrease was 16 per cent and in the 6 states west of the river it was 8 per cent. Nebraska was the only state where there was any increase, with all other states having decreases except Minnesota, where there was no change.

In the western states there was a decrease of about 13,000 head or 4 per cent in the number of cattle on feed January 1 this year from a year earlier. For the 10 states included, four, Colorado, Arizona, Nevada and California had increases and five, Montana, Wyoming, Utah, Idaho and Oregon, had decreases. The number of cattle fed in the Lancaster, Pennsylvania, area this winter will probably not be much more than half the number a year ago, with a decrease of around 30,000 head.

The number of cattle on feed for market January 1 this year was the smallest since 1921 and probably the smallest since 1916. The decrease this year was due to the short corn crop of 1930, to the heavy losses suffered by many feeders in 1929, to the difficulties in financing feeding operations this year in some sections, and to the relatively small supply of feeding cattle available at markets.

Total shipments of stocker and feeder cattle into the eleven Corn Belt states for the 6 months, July to December, were 10 per cent smaller this year than last and second smallest for the period since 1921. Shipments during the first three months of the period were very small, but beginning with October they tended to increase relatively, and the shipments during the last three months were the largest proportion of the 6 months movement on record, with shipments in December the largest for the month since 1923.

Feeder shipments in 1930 included an unusually large proportion of feeder calves. While total feeder shipments from 4 leading markets were 17 per cent smaller during the last half of the year than for the same period in 1929, calf shipments were actually 9 per cent larger and made up over 20 per cent of the total while in 1929 they made up only 16 per cent and in 1928 only 9 per cent. Shipments of stocker and feeder cows and heifers decreased materially, both as a proportion of the total and also in actual head.

Reports of feeders as to kinds and weights of cattle on feed also point to a relatively large proportion of calves and light weight steers. Reports as to time of marketing indicate that the proportion of numbers on feed January 1 this year to be marketed from January to March was not much different from the proportion reported on January 1, 1930. Actual marketings during these 3 months in 1930 were relatively small. All present indications point to a small market supply of fed cattle during the first few months of 1931.

The estimated number of cattle on feed January 1, 1931 in the different states of the Corn Belt as a percentage of the number January 1, 1930 is as follows:

First page of the crop report letter reviewed by Jacob Vermeer on January 19, 1931. The letter begins by discussing the cattle market.

quarters. By the time Dad and all his siblings attended, this one-room country schoolhouse had moved half a mile north.

In 1939, Jacob bought some Pella National Bank shares from his brother-in-law, Art Van Donselaar. Then in 1945, Jacob was elected to the board of directors of Pella National Bank. In a 1947 document—the year which marked the ninety-seventh anniversary of the original Pella Savings Institution—Jacob G. Vermeer is listed as a director. In 1951, he resigned from the board for health reasons.

Jacob's influence on Dad's farming habits was immense. From Jacob, Dad learned that a good farmer keeps his farm neat and orderly. Dad often judged how good a farmer was by the tidiness of his farmstead. From Jacob, he learned that farming meant making wise decisions to improve the farm-land by tiling it. Dad first learned how to tile the wet spots

From a 1947 Pella National Bank Brochure

"In over ninety-seven years of operation, this banking institution has helped, aided, and assisted thousands of people to acquire their farms, homes, and businesses: and it is interesting to note that the descendants of our first customers and pioneers comprise a large percentage of those who transact their banking business with us today. As we start our ninety-eighth year in the same location, Iowa's second oldest banking institution is confident of the future. It has faith and confidence in the people of this community and of its institutions. We welcome the opportunity to serve the people of this community, whose business and good will has made the success of this institution possible."[1]

Gary working with horses on the family farm

using horses to make the trench. Then he went one step further: One of the early Vermeer company products was a power take-off (PTO) tiling trencher. Dad had helped his father tile the land with horses, so he knew from hard experience that there must be a better way to do this job.

In addition to being a good farmer, Dad and his brothers grew up with a father who was kind and considerate toward others who were going through difficult times. On some farmland Jacob owned, there was a vacant, dilapidated brick house. Previously, the bachelor who lived in it had kept chickens upstairs and pigs on the main floor. In 1932, during the difficult Depression years, a man named John Gezel went to the Vermeer home.

"Jake," he said, "I want to rent that house."

Gary picking corn

Jacob answered, "I won't rent it. It isn't livable. I am going to burn it down."

Two weeks later, John came to Jacob again and said he was willing to fix up the house. He said he desperately needed a place to live with his family. This time Jacob agreed. As rent payment, John would work for Jacob several days a month.

The Gezels did indeed fix up that property, and it was occupied for several decades.

When that house was burned down in the mid-1950s, I was a young girl. I remember it burning, as well as the story that animals had lived in it and that it was later fixed up by tenants. Jacob's sensitivity to people who could use a little assistance left its mark on Dad and his brothers.

Jacob and Anna's wedding photo

Until he was thirty-five, Jacob Vermeer was a bachelor. As a single adult, he enjoyed farming with his father, Gerrit, and socializing with his Vermeer cousins. One of those cousins, Otto Vermeer, married Dena Stadt from Grand Rapids, Michigan, in 1911. In 1916, Dena's good friend Anna Haven came from Grand Rapids to visit— and Jacob met Anna. The match was made, and they were married on August 23, 1917, in Anna's home in Grand Rapids. She was twenty-two; he was thirty-five.

Marsha Jansen Overbergen, the daughter of Jacob's youngest sister Mattie, remembers Jacob especially well. She says Jacob was kind, quiet, and thoughtful with his nieces and nephews. When Mattie's husband passed away at a young age, Jacob helped his sister out. Marsha recalls coming home from school and sometimes seeing Uncle Jake and her mother sitting at the kitchen table, drinking coffee and going through bills together. Uncle Jake advised her mother on financial matters. He was very willing to share his financial expertise with his family. In the last years of Jacob's life, he and Anna lived in Pella, just a few houses away from Mattie and her daughters, Evelyn and Marsha.

Jacob Vermeer with sons Dutch, Gary, John, and Harry

Dad also learned punctuality from his father. Jacob always ate "dinner" (noon meal) and "supper" (evening meal) at precisely 11:30 a.m. and 5:30 p.m. Dad continued that very regular schedule for meals every year he was part of the leadership team at Vermeer. He came home for dinner at 11:30. He often took a power nap after dinner before returning to work either on the farm or at the factory. And we always ate an early supper at 5:30.

As long as they lived, my parents used the terms "dinner" and "supper" for the noon and evening meals, respectively. After Dad died, Mom spent the last years of her life at Fairhaven East, a Pella retirement home. Even at Fairhaven, the residents called their noon meal "dinner." Many of them were retired farmers who had eaten their main meal at noon, and they continued using that terminology in their retirement years.

Like his father, Dad was a stickler about timeliness. If he said the departure time for a Vermeer flight to a customer or dealer was 7:00 a.m., he meant the plane was taking off at 7:00 a.m. I have heard legends of people arriving at the airport at 7:00, only to see the plane taxiing down the runway for takeoff. These stories might be true, or they might be myths. In my research, I did not find anyone who was *actually* left behind. Regardless, it is certainly true that Gary wanted people to be timely!

Steve Haverly, a long-term co-worker of Gary, remembers, "Being on time meant at least five to ten minutes before the departure time. The rule of thumb was not to be the last person there, ever!"

John Vander Wert, another long-term colleague, remembers Gary's thoughts on timeliness this way: "You could never be 'on time.' You were either early, or you were late! So to be on time, you should be there five to ten minutes early."

When coaching new Vermeer team members, John cautioned them, "I suggest you never make Gary late."

The story of one employee who could never seem to get to the office by the 7:00 a.m. starting time has become legendary. After several tardy arrivals, Dad asked him, "If we set start time at 8:00 a.m., could you make it on time then?"

The employee said, very honestly, "Gary, I am not sure."

Timeliness was so ingrained into Dad that he never did understand that answer.

My brother, Bob, remembers hearing punctuality stories about Jacob and Anna. When Jacob was in the car, ready to leave for an appointment he simply left without Anna if she wasn't on time.

That sense of timeliness has affected subsequent generation as well. Both my brothers and I are generally very punctual. The timeliness tradition has continued as our family has grown and spouses of children and grandchildren have joined the clan. For example, gathering at the family camp north of Pella became a traditional event. Sometimes my husband, Dale, and my nephew-in-law, Chad Quist, drove the sixty miles from Des Moines to join the gathering. Both had jobs that kept them in Des Moines until they had finished seeing patients. After their last appointment, they would rush to Pella. They sometimes arrived to find that the meal had begun—on time and without them!

Dad's love of hunting also came from his father. At age eight, he received an air rifle from Jacob. Jacob had received the same gift from his father, Gerrit, at an early age. Jacob

Jacob with grandson Stan Vermeer

taught Dad, "If you hunt, you eat your game." So when Dad and his brothers shot pigeons on the farm, their mom made pigeon soup.

After my parents married, Mom was a great sport about cooking the game Dad shot. She learned how to fix squirrel, rabbit, duck, goose, deer, moose, elk, and anything else he bagged. My parents often shared wild game with groups of people who appreciated hunting and eating the game—hunter friends, neighbors, family, and members of their church. Mom's typical recipe included lots of mushroom soup, which improved the flavor and tenderized the wild meat.

Jacob encouraged all his sons in pursuing their interests. Uncle John, who founded Pella Nursery two miles east of Pella, said his love for plants started at a young age. Then, as a teenager, he became interested in peanut plants and wondered why no one grew peanuts in Iowa. He decided to experiment, and he planted several peanut seeds. That year, he had a bumper crop. One plant he dug up was especially huge with peanuts. Jacob was so fascinated by the size of his son's peanut plant that he took it along to one of his Pella National Bank board meetings. He showed the other board members that, yes, you can grow peanuts in Iowa!

Dad and his brothers were curious about many different topics, and their parents modeled and encouraged this curiosity. Uncle John told me that in the upstairs southwest bedroom was a closet with shelves packed with children's books. Jacob, whose extensive reading included the daily newspaper, read these books to his sons.

When I asked Uncle John about discipline in the family as he was growing up, he quickly responded that his mother had done most of the discipline in their household. With a smile on his face, he said, "I think my dad had a hard time punishing us because he had been quite a prankster himself growing up."

Dad and his brothers inherited Jacob's pleasure in pranks. All four of them walked daily to Plainview Country School. They often carried slingshots with them and shot rabbits, which were a nuisance for farmers and not considered edible.

One afternoon while walking home from school, Gary, Dutch, and John decided to test their slingshot accuracy on the insulators atop the twelve-foot telephone poles alongside the road. They succeeded in hitting their targets quite consistently.

The next day, Wally Fowler, owner of the telephone company, made a stop at their country school. "Many company insulators atop the telephone poles near the school have been broken," he said. "We want to know who did this."

He paused, and then continued, "It's very strange that the trail of broken insulators begins at the school and ends at the Vermeer farm."

He then told the three shamefaced Vermeer brothers that their slingshot target practice must stop immediately. It did.

Insulators

With many telephone and electric wires moving underground, insulators have become a collectors' item. *Collectors Weekly* describes them this way: "Insulators were originally designed to keep the wires holding telegraphs and telephones insulated from the wooden poles that held them aloft. In conjunction with the expansion of rural electrification in the early 20th century, there was a major boom in the manufacturing of insulators, peaking from the 1920s through the 1940s with production in the millions per year."[2]

The brothers practiced other, more deliberate, roadside pranks as well. Uncle John told me about taking an old tire or a woman's purse, tying it to a string or rope, and putting it in the middle of the road. The brothers then hid in the ditch behind a hedge. When a car stopped to move the tire or pick up the purse, the boys yanked it back into the ditch while the driver was getting out of the vehicle. From behind the hedge, they grinned as the driver stared in puzzlement at the empty road and then drove on.

Tudor, one of the Vermeer cousins who was known to be quite mischievous, also tried this prank. But when the driver walked toward the ditch instead of back to his car, Tudor took off through the cornfield, hearing his pursuer behind him for an entire mile. He was safely home before he realized that his own passage through the corn field had made the corn rustle—a noise he had thought was an angry pursuer.

Jacob and Anna Vermeer with their five oldest grandchildren. From left to right: Tom, Stan, Mary, Richard, and Bob.

EARLIER GENERATIONS: GRANDFATHER GERRIT AND GREAT-GRANDFATHER BRANT

Like Dad, his grandfather, Gerrit Vermeer, enjoyed hunting, walking, and teasing the grandchildren. Gerrit and his twin brother, Anthonie, came to Iowa from the Netherlands at age thirteen, along with their parents, Brant and Teunetje; older stepbrother, Otto; and younger brother, Hendrick.

During their trip to Iowa, eleven-year-old Hendrick, who spoke only Dutch, fell behind the group near Montezuma. *Vermeer Family History* records the event:

> *Setting out alone in hope of overtaking the group traveling with the oxen, he came to a crossroad and took the wrong trail. He soon discovered that he was lost and gripped with fear, he frantically ran all day until he overtook a company of American travelers. The poor lad was unable to communicate his plight to them, but one of them surmising that he belonged*

Brothers Anthonie, Gerrit (Gary's grandfather), and Hendrick Vermeer

to the company of Dutch trekkers and knowing the course of their journey, restored him to his anxious parents.[3]

Gerrit married Hendrika De Bruin on April 23, 1874, and she died twenty-one years later, leaving him with six children. Mattie, the youngest, was only five. The family had just built a new barn on the homestead, and they held her funeral in that barn. Mattie lived with him until he passed away twenty-eight years later.

In 1917, when Jacob married and took over the homestead, Gerrit and Mattie moved to Pella. They lived at the corner of Washington and East First Street. They sometimes walked to the homestead—which was located at the site of the current Pella Nursery—and visited with relatives along the way.

Gerrit and Mattie were also known for riding about town in a sporty Kissel touring car in which they gave rides to grandchil-

Gerrit Vermeer   *Hendrika Vermeer*

dren. A very popular Kissel model was the "Gold Bug" speed-ster. This was likely the model Gerrit drove in the early 1920s.

A photocopied family history says that one of Jacob's sons remembers at age three going on an outing in the Kissel with Grandfather Gerrit, Aunt Mattie, and Jacob during which Jacob shot a red-tailed hawk out of a large elm tree at the side of the road. Although the history does not identify the child by name, that three-year-old was probably Dad.

Kissel Motor Car Company: A Brief Blooming

The White Way Auto Company in Pella sold the Kissel Kar line, along with Buicks and Oldsmobiles.[4] Founded in Hartford, Wisconsin, in 1906, the Kissel Motor Car Company built custom, high-quality automobiles. During World War I, the company produced trucks and ambu-lances for the United States military. For a time after the war, the company prospered, but with stiff competi-tion and the Great Depression, it foundered and filed for receivership protection at the end of 1930.[5]

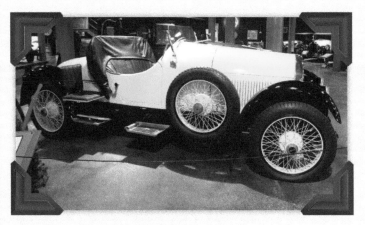

The Kissel Gold Bug Speedster

Jacob continued in Gerrit's footsteps and used new modes of transportation, such as a 1928 Chevy. Uncle John recalls Jacob having a keen interest in new technologies. John also remembers the family farm always being equipped with a new tractor, even though Jacob enjoyed farming with horses more than with a tractor.

Jacob's first tractor was a Huber. In 2007, when Dad went to the Harold Warp Pioneer Village in Minden, Nebraska, he found a similar Huber tractor and sat there for some time with his memories of it.

Dad updated cars every few years. He always bought locally, and it was usually a Chevy or a Ford. Besides keeping his cars current, he also enjoyed using up-to-date equipment on his farm. He followed a similar philosophy for his factory. He believed it was important to update his capital investments in the manufacturing plants. His father's and his grandfather's influence continued, in both his business and personal life.

Gary and his brothers by their 1928 Chevy

The grandchildren of Gerrit Vermeer were all close friends. Gary is in the back row on the left.

Jacob and Anna Vermeer with sons, left to right: John, Gary, Harry, and Dutch (Elmer)

INFLUENCES FROM MICHIGAN: THE HAVEN FAMILY

Gary was also influenced by his mother Anna Haven Vermeer's parents, John and Elsie Haven. Uncle John remembers a family trip to Michigan to visit them. Because his youngest brother, Harry, appears to be about three in a family photo taken at the time, Uncle John was able to date that trip to 1932 or 1933. That was the last time Uncle John saw his maternal grandparents.

Dad's maternal grandfather, John Haven, was an architect and contractor in Grand Rapids, Michigan. Records of many of his projects have been lost, but we do know that one of his bigger projects was a furniture museum near downtown Grand Rapids.

No doubt Anna's architect-and-contractor father suggested Jacob and Anna put in modern facilities when they built a home in 1925. In their new construction, they installed both an in indoor bathroom and a Delco system for electricity.

Five years later, on October 9, 1930, a *Pella Chronicle* headline read, "Rural Homes to have Electric Light Service." The article declared:

> *Rural dwellers east of Pella will in a comparatively short time be sitting under the glow of a light and operate electric irons and washers and other appliances on current furnished by the city, following the action of the city Council Tuesday Night…*
>
> *As means to speedy action in this work, it was voted to order a carload of poles and 2,000 pounds of wire.*[6]

However, the "speedy action" required two years to deliver electricity to Jacob and Anna's home two miles east of Pella. All the work was done by hand, so it was very labor inten-

Grandpa John and Grandma Elsie Haven with their Iowa grandsons in Grand Rapids, Michigan, in the early 1930s

sive. Watching some of these labor-intensive projects probably spurred Dad's later inventive ability to mechanize processes.

It was quite an advantage that the Vermeer household had these luxuries in the 1930s. Mom, who grew up an additional two miles east of the Vermeer family, did not have rural electricity or indoor plumbing until she and Dad married. The *Pella Chronicle* article does reveal one reason for the delay in providing electricity further east. At the end of the Vermeer farm was the county line, and "the connection beyond the Marion county line cannot be made until a franchise is secured."[7]

When our daughter, Mindi, and her husband, Frank, lived in Grand Rapids, Dad and Mom sometimes traveled to visit them. On one visit, Dad really wanted to see the home where his mother had grown up. He remembered childhood visits to his maternal grandparents, and he remembered they lived somewhere on Leonard Street. On one trip to Frank and Mindi, Dad decided to find that house. They all got in the car and traveled along Leonard Street. Dad was able to identify his grandparents' house—exactly what he had set out to do.

As the eldest son of Jacob and Anna Vermeer, Dad did spend some time with his grandfather, Gerrit Vermeer, and also with the Haven grandparents in Michigan. Nevertheless, by far the most influential person in his life as he grew up was his father. Jacob died in 1952 at age seventy, when I was two years old.

My only memory of him—a very faint one—is of sitting on his lap on the porch of his Pella home. I wish I could have known him. Based on what others have told me, he was a kind, learned, entrepreneurial, community-oriented, and fun-loving person. As was his son.

In 1992, when Dad was inducted into the Junior Achievement Business Hall of Fame, he made a few comments

Gary with fellow Junior Achievement award recipients

Gary being inducted into the Junior Achievement Business Hall of Fame in 1992

at the awards dinner. His comments reflected his great appreciation for his ancestors. I remember him saying this:

My great-grandfather, Brant Vermeer, came to Iowa in 1856. He found that Iowa was a land of opportunity. His son, Gerrit, my grandfather, also was able to farm and help each of his children own their own farms. My father, Jacob, even got a law degree and used it to write up legal documents for friends and relatives. My dad found Iowa to be a place of opportunity.

Although I started out farming, I was able to start and grow a manufacturing business. Just as Iowa has been a state of opportunity for my ancestors, I hope that it will continue to be a place of opportunity for my children and grandchildren and for all the young people in the state of Iowa.

Gary with his immediate family at the Junior Achievement banquet

2 | Equality

Opportunities Provided for a Daughter

Historians have described the 1950s as "booming"—the era of a booming economy, booming suburbs, and especially, a baby boom. Between 1946 and 1964, 77 million babies were born in the United States, and I am among them.[1] Born on November 22, 1949, I am on the leading edge of the Baby Boomer Generation. I was born exactly one year after Dad incorporated Vermeer Manufacturing.

Dad holding me, circa 1950

The 1950s—the decade of my childhood—was an era of stereotyped roles. Men earned money, and, once married, women worked at home as wives and mothers. Mom was one of those women, fulfilling that traditional role with grace and generosity. Growing up under her care, I planned to go to college and thought I would go into education or nursing, the two traditional occupations chosen by women in that era.

In that day, women did not become CEOs. Even as recently as 1972, Katherine Graham was the only female CEO of a Fortune 500 company.[2] When my husband, Dale, attended medical school in the 1970s, he recalls that just 5 percent of the medical students were women.

Although I grew up surrounded by these separated gender roles, Dad never gave me the impression that there was a glass ceiling for me because I was a woman. Assimilating his belief as my own, I was strengthened to pursue opportunities unhampered by stereotyped gender roles.

FAMILY INHERITANCE IN THE DUTCH TRADITION

Equal treatment of women has definite Dutch historic roots. The first stockholder of the Dutch East Indies Company, founded in the Netherlands in 1602, was a woman.[3] Dutch women could own property and inherit property when their husbands died, but this was not the case for English women.

In more recent history in the Netherlands, it has been very typical for Dutch families to divide the farmland between all the children. Through the years, this has meant that farms are continually divided into smaller and smaller tracts of land. This has necessitated land swaps in order for present owners to have contiguous plots of land. Shrinking farm sizes due to the division of land among all the offspring may have been part of the reason many Dutch immigrated to America, Canada, South Africa, Indonesia, and the Caribbean.

The tradition of inheritance equality for women was evident in my Dutch ancestors. My great-great-grandfather, Brant Vermeer, who immigrated with his wife and four sons, willed all his property to his "lawfully wedded wife Teunetje." If Teunetje remarried after his death, she would retain one-third of his property, and the rest would be divided equally among his three sons and stepson.

My great-grandfather, Gerrit Vermeer, gave land to each of his children. His five daughters all received land. Jacob, the only son, received the family farm (the homestead).

Perhaps in part because of this egalitarian Dutch heritage, Dad gave equal gifts of Vermeer Manufacturing stock to both male and female descendants. He began by giving equal stock gifts to Bob, Stan, and me when I was eleven. He continued giving annual stock gifts to his descendants of both genders until his death in 2009.

Estate of Brant Vermeer	Transcript certified by the Clerk of the District Court in and for Marion County, Iowa, January 18, 1901 filed in the office of the District Court in and for Mahaska County, Iowa, January 23, 1901 and entered at length in Will Record C, page 374.

Certifies that due notice of probation was had and that the will of Brant Vermeer was probated in Marion County, Iowa, June 3, 1873 in words and figures as follows:

"I, Brand Vermeer, a native of the Kingdom of the NETHERLANDS now a resident of the County of Mahaska and State of Iowa, being in full possession of a sound mind and memory knowing the frailty of this transitory life do hereby make, ordain and publish this my last will and testament, revoking all former wills made by me or under my directions. I give and bequeath the whole of my estate both real and personal to my lawful wedded wife Teunetje Vermeer who shall have and hold the same, derive all the benefits therefrom; shall have power to sell any or all portion of the personal property, but the real estate shall not be sold nor conveyed unless necessary for the support of my children. In case my said wife, after my decease shall marry again, and by so doing, should cease to be my widow, she shall only be entitled to retain one-third of my property, and the remainder to be set aside to be divided among my children when they become of age, as follows: My stepson Otto Pothoven shall received one-fourth part of my personal property, so remaining, as his full and his entire portion of my estate. My three sons, Gerrit, Anthony and Hendrick Vermeer shall be entitled each to one-fourth of my personal property and one-third of my real estate. The same rule will also be observed and be acted upon in dividing the estate after my wife's decease, if she shall die still being my widow. I do further appoint my wife as Administrator of my estate after my decease and she shall not be required when entering upon the discharge of that duty to give any bond or security whatever.

In witness whereof I have hereunto set my hand this 29th day of November A.D., 1859."

B. Vermeer

(Duly Witnessed)

Brant Vermeer's will, which stated that all his property would go to his wife

WOMEN IN CHURCH LEADERSHIP

When it came to church leadership, though, my Dutch Reformed heritage was not egalitarian.

Once, when I ventured to suggest I might attend seminary instead of becoming a nurse or teacher, Mom quickly reminded me, "Mary, women don't become preachers." Neither did they become elders or deacons in their congregations. Mom held the viewpoint of most of her contemporaries, both men and women.

Dad, however, was ahead of his time on this matter. Once, when he and Mom and I were seated around our kitchen table, he explained his views on women becoming deacons or elders in the Christian Reformed Church.

He said to us, "It's only a matter of time before women serve as elders and deacons in our churches." In the 1950s, that was not a common or accepted viewpoint in our denomination! Dad sometimes told us that when he was young, the church believed women should cover their heads when attending church. By the 1950s, that was no longer considered a required, biblical practice. So he was quite sure that in the future women would be elders and deacons in the church as well. He was not an outspoken advocate for this, but he was open-minded about how things would change in the future.

LEARNING TO HUNT AND FLY

Dad's love of hunting, which began with that gift of a gun at age eight, continued as a pastime throughout his entire life. He shared that pastime with his sons—and with me. My father saw no reason why his daughter should not be involved in hunting with him. When I was in sixth grade, he let me use a 410 over/under shotgun—the only gun I ever used—and took me hunting with him. We hunted together when I was in junior high and high school. Year-round we trudged through various timber properties, hunting squirrels. In the fall hunting season, he drove to our duck blind north of Pella to hunt ducks and geese. I enjoyed hunting and really liked tramping through the woods and sitting in the duck blind with Dad.

When I was thirteen, Vermeer Manufacturing owned an airplane, a two-seat Piper Cub. Dad—and some of the company management and sales staff—had a private pilot's licenses and used the Piper Cub to make customer visits. Dad thought it would be good if my brothers and I had chances to fly with him in the two-seater and take control of the plane once it was in the air.

One holiday break, when my brothers were home from college, we all got that opportunity. We went out to a grass strip south of Pella, the original Pella airport, which had been a military training strip during World War II. It was the same strip where Dad had learned to fly in 1949. Dad gave each of us a turn taking control of the plane. I don't remember the order in which we took turns, but I do remember that when my turn came, I loved it.

After the flight, Dad asked me, "Would you like to take lessons and learn to fly?"

I answered with an instant and eager, "Yes!"

So, at fifteen, I began taking flying lessons at the airport in Oskaloosa, logging eleven hours of flying time. As soon as I turned sixteen and could legally do so, I started flying solo. That summer, I worked in a Vermeer Manufacturing office each morning, then drove to the Oskaloosa airport in the afternoon for more flight instruction and solo flying. I also did ground school there, prepared for the written test, and passed it.

That fall, I continued to practice my flying skills. On my seventeenth birthday, the first day I was eligible for a private license, I went to Des Moines for my check ride with the Federal Aviation Agency (FAA). I passed.

I continued to fly for several years, logging more than two hundred hours of flight time. My brothers, Bob and Stan, also received their private pilots' licenses. Of the three siblings, Stan flew the most over the years, accumulating close to one thousand hours of flight time.

Some of my two hundred hours were logged when I was an attendant for the Tulip Court for Pella's thirty-third annual Tulip Time in 1968. Pella's Tulip Queen, Judy De Cook, and her court made many visits around the state of Iowa, promoting Pella and the May Tulip Time festival. As a licensed pilot, I

The Tulip Queen and court prepare for their flight.

flew the members of the court to Cedar Rapids, Ottumwa, Des Moines, and—for the first court exchange ever—to Orange City, Iowa, for its annual Tulip Festival.

Dad escorting me at the Tulip Time Evening Program

The Orange City trip was Dad's idea. In 1968, there was no tradition of exchanges between the Tulip Time Courts of Orange City and Pella. But the festivals were on different weekends, so it was very possible for each town to host the queen and court of the other town during their festivals. Dad thought it would be a nice event to exchange courts. So a week after the Pella festival, I flew the court to Orange City. It has now become a tradition, and all the subsequent courts have made this exchange. However, the 1968 Pella royalty were the only ones—so far—to be piloted by a court member!

Those first years, I made several trips with Dad; I was in the left lead pilot seat, and he flew right seat. That arrangement was often a learning experience for me.

Landings are a big part of learning to fly. Flaring out is lifting the nose in the last part of the landing process. Pulling back on the yoke (control mechanism) too early can stall out the airplane and produce a very abrupt contact with the runway during landing.

While landing on a trip to visit Bob in San Antonio, Texas, where he was stationed as a member of the National Guard,

I pulled back the yoke too early. The plane flared out high above the runway.

Dad quickly pushed down the yoke and helped me land the plane, preventing a hard landing.

When we had taxied to a stop, he said very calmly, "You flared out too high." And that typical, calm statement was the full extent of his coaching in response to my mistake.

I learned another lesson from him when I flew the Beechcraft Bonanza up to Baudette, Minnesota. On Canadian fishing trips, we needed a seaplane. So we typically landed the Bonanza in Baudette and picked up the seaplane for Canadian water landings. On the return flight, we landed the seaplane in Baudette and transferred back to the Bonanza.

On one flight to Canada, I failed to properly turn off the Bonanza switches. Its batteries were dead when we wanted to make our return flight. We waited while the battery recharged and then continued back to Pella.

Once we were airborne, Dad matter-of-factly told me, "It's a good idea to always double-check to be sure the switches are off." That ended his lesson.

However, like his other instructions, it was a lesson I did not forget.

In 1982, I was working to get current with my flying when I began working full-time for Vermeer Manufacturing. I needed to log one thousand hours in order to be certified for our planes. I logged just over two hundred hours before I began work, and my job made accumulating another eight hundred hours of flight time nearly impossible. At the same time, insurance rates for corporate aircraft skyrocketed, so I decided to become a non-current pilot instead of working for certification. But I have continued to enjoy flying right seat with other pilots.

EQUAL OPPORTUNITY IN THE WORKPLACE

In 2012, when I chaired the National Association of Manufacturing, I spoke at the Detroit Economic Club. After the event, a woman my age approached me. With tears in her eyes, she told me, "I was never invited to be part of our family construction company." Several of her brothers, however, had been invited, and now the business was not doing well. She believed some of her skill sets would have been helpful in the family business, but she had not been given the option of participating.

Through the years, I have met other women who grew up in families that owned businesses and have told me they regret not being part of those businesses. Why did they not become part of the family businesses? Because in their families, sons were expected to be involved in the business, but not the daughters. This was particularly true in construction and industrial companies.

I am forever grateful that Dad treated me as my brothers' equal and did not limit my career options as a woman.

When I was in seventh grade, my parents planned a three-month trip around the world, sightseeing, visiting missionaries of our church, and stopping to see business contacts. Both of my brothers were already away at college. I told Dad I would like to go along on that trip.

He replied, "In the future, if you become part of the business, you will be able to take trips like this."

I was, of course, disappointed. In my disappointment, I didn't realize the significance of his signal that it would be fine for me, his daughter, to become part of the family business. He was, of course, correct about the travel opportunities. During my tenure at Vermeer Corporation, I have been able to travel within the United States and to other countries, supporting our dealers and customers around the world.

WOMEN IN THE WORKPLACE: TODAY AND TOMORROW

The issue of women in the workforce continues to get a lot of attention. Women's participation in the workforce around the world is 50 percent, while men's participation is 82 percent.

Women have made strides since 1972. In 2017, the percentage is still small, but instead of just one there are thirty-two women who hold CEO positions in Fortune 500 companies.[4] The number of women pursuing higher education has also increased; this achievement accounts for 50 percent of the economic growth in Organization for Economic Cooperation and Development (OECD) countries in the past fifty years and has the potential to increase growth in G20 countries as well.[5]

The B20 Task Force on Employment wrestles with these issues and the recommendations for greater participation of women in the workforce.

Since 2015, I have been part of the B20—the business leaders who give recommendations to G20 leaders, or the group of twenty nations that comprise 85 percent of the world economy. I have been able to continue in Dad's footsteps, helping provide workplace opportunities for other women.

The digitization of the world is likely to have an impact on women and their inclusion in the workforce. An Intel survey of 2,200 women in India, Mexico, Uganda, and Egypt revealed that 77 percent of women used the internet to further their education, 54 percent used it for financial services and banking.[6] The digital economy allows men and women to start and grow small businesses. These entrepreneurs can get financing online, learn about markets, and take online training courses.

I believe the opportunities for women are bright. Although there are still gaps in certain areas of our economy, especially in STEM (Science, Technology, Engineering, and Math) fields, there are many programs that will help narrow that gap in the future. In Iowa, we are seeing positive trends due to the efforts and focus of many educators in our state and of the Governor's STEM Council. We are seeing that more girls become interested in STEM careers when they have been involved in STEM scale-up programs. Scale-up programs are specific courses geared toward getting young people excited about STEM learning and careers.

One of Dad's defining qualities was his acceptance of women as equals. As his daughter, I am grateful to have benefitted from that defining quality, and I believe he would be pleased with the strides women have made since his death in 2009.

A SALUTE TO MOM

Although in my professional life I have been greatly shaped by Dad, Mom has had an equal influence, especially on my family and personal life. She merits my acknowledging her generous life and her formative role in mine.

Mom grew up as Matilda Van Gorp, the middle-born of the five children of John and Minnie Blom Van Gorp. She was raised on a farm five miles east of Pella. Born on February 14, 1920, she attended Wheatgrow, a country school similar to the one Dad went to. Later, my two brothers, Stan and Bob, both attended Wheatgrow for their initial grade-school years.

Mom's family attended the same church as Dad's, First Christian Reformed Church of Pella. Dad often described the beginning of their relationship this way: "I spotted this good-looking young girl across the church. Then I found out she was only thirteen, and I had to wait until she was sixteen to date her!"

They did start dating when Mom was sixteen, and they married on her twenty-first birthday, February 14, 1941. She was required

Matilda and Gary's wedding photo

by her father to be twenty-one before she married, and she obeyed! Dad, with his usual practical bent, said he ended up with a good deal: He could celebrate his wife's birthday, their anniversary, and Valentine's Day all with one big party!

In Mom's values, her family ranked second only to her faith. With her children, she was very fair, and she loved interacting with each of us. After we became adults, she enjoyed inviting us for lunch or coffee time. She knew just which foods each of us liked and often prepared those special dishes. She knew that I loved creamed chicken over mashed potatoes and *snijboontjes* (thin-sliced green beans). These dishes were preparation-intensive. To make creamed chicken, she boiled the chicken, deboned it, cut it in small pieces, and then creamed it. Her mashed potatoes, too, were made from scratch. Green beans from her garden (and later from the farmers' market) were sliced in the French cut slicer and then canned.

For many decades, for the birthdays of each of her children and their spouses, she made our favorite pies from scratch. My favorite pie was chocolate French silk with a meringue crust. Dale's favorite was sour cream raisin pie. As we became adults with families of our own, we appreciated even more her work and her love in preparing our favorite foods.

Mom also was generous and giving for people outside our family. She shared generously the produce from her farm garden. In later life, she often drove widowed church members to appointments. Sometimes she was older than the person she was transporting!

She modeled a vibrant spiritual walk by her daily devotions each morning at the kitchen table. Mom prayed daily for each of her children and grandchildren, and later her great-grandchildren. She was a frequent church volunteer. One year, she and I taught a kindergarten Bible school class together.

When we were at college, Mom was faithful in writing weekly letters to us. She continued faithfully writing letters to her grandchildren after they graduated from Pella Christian High School. She wrote to us about current Pella events—and always included a note about the weather. A true farmer's wife, even after Vermeer Corporation overshadowed their farm life, she and Dad remained tuned in to the unpredictable Iowa weather and its impact on crops. I don't recall ever receiving a letter from Dad. If he wanted to communicate, he telephoned.

Remembering people's names and details about their lives was one of her strengths. She often helped Dad with these details, speedily remembering people's names at social events. She was the parent who remembered the dates of clan birthdays and anniversaries, and she planned the celebration of those events. Her taking this responsibility left it to Dad to remember just two items: her birthday and their anniversary. Not a hard task, considering that both were on the same day.

Mom was also the family disciplinarian. She said she spanked Stan, but a strong word was sufficient with Bob. She punished me by putting me in a closet, and I like to blame those penalties for my claustrophobia. However, sometimes she used the entry closet, which had no door. It was similar to the current discipline of "time out," which Dale and I also used for our own children

In the early 1990s, at Bob's suggestion, the Vermeer clan started to work with a family consulting group to plan for the future of the family business. As part of that process, all eight Vermeer grandchildren, who ranged in age from junior high school through college, were interviewed individually. The psychologist who did those interviews told us that, remarkably, all eight of the grandchildren said they never wanted to disappoint their grandmother. They might disappoint their parents or grandfather—but not their grandmother. Their response indicates the love and respect in the heart of each of Mom's descendants.

In recent years, Dale has been researching our ancestry, and he discovered that Mom was descended from royalty through her maternal grandfather, Engle Blom. Mom's ancestors include the king of the Netherlands Floris V, Eleanor of Aquitaine, and King Henry II. Going even further back— eighty generations—Mom's line also includes Charlemagne and Caesar Augustus. Mom died in July 2014, before we ever learned about her ancestry, and I don't think she would have found these facts easy to believe. She was the essence of humility, putting her husband, family, and friends before herself.

Although she would have poo-poohed any royal ancestry, even without it she was our family queen, choosing the traditional women's role of her era and influencing the personal lives of her children, grand-children, and great-grand-children in profound ways.

Matilda Vermeer

Matilda with her children, grandchildren, and great-grandchildren in 2013

3 | Skeptical and Curious

Always Searching and Learning

Dad was a man with restless energy and an avid curiosity, but he was skeptical about academia and advanced degrees.

In the mid-1990s, Dad was interviewed for *Iowa Pride,* a book about Iowa entrepreneurs. From that time on, he often used that book to illustrate his viewpoint on formal education because more than half of the inventors and entrepreneurs featured in that book had only a high school education. "You don't need an advanced degree to be successful, especially in innovation," he said. "You can't educate imagination." Sometimes he went so far as to say that college could squelch a creative spirit.

FRIENDSHIPS WITH COLLEGE PRESIDENTS

Paradoxically, despite his opinions about advanced degrees, he enjoyed the company of academic leaders, three of them college presidents.

Dad's friendship with Ken Weller, Central College president from 1970 to 1990, began during a Pella Community Hospital fundraising campaign. A creative fundraiser, Dad hired Ken to consult at Vermeer in exchange for Ken's donation to the hospital. Ken had been an economics professor at Hope College before coming to Central. Dad admired Ken's ability to take his theoretical knowledge and make it prac-

Iowa Pride

In 1996, Iowa State University published *Iowa Pride*, by Duane Schmidt, featuring sixty-one Iowans who have had a global impact. Dad was one of them. Schmidt used the following criteria in making his selection:

- Worldwide recognition
- Tangible notability
- A patent of overwhelming significance
- A development of an industry
- A Hall of Fame selection
- A world prize, such as the Nobel
- A national award, such as an Oscar, Emmy, or Pulitzer Prize

Besides Dad, others on the list were:

- John Vincent Atanasoff, who invented the digital computer
- Roy Carver, who created the tire retread
- George Gallup, who developed sampling methods
- W.A. Jennings, who invented a portable concrete form
- Fred Maytag, who developed the agitator washing machine
- Walter Sheaffer, who invented the first practical self-filling fountain pen
- Jane Smiley, a Pulitzer Prize-winning author
- Henry Wallace, who pioneered hybrid seed corn
- F.A. Wittern, who invented the change-giving vending machine
- Grant Wood, America's painter laureate

The book also includes a list of "Iowans Who Made It Elsewhere" and a list of "Iowa Firsts."

Schmidt said he grew in his love for Iowa as he learned Iowans' stories. "As the years have whizzed by in the preparation of this book, my esteem for Iowa has soared. I hope your appreciation of this beautiful land and its people grows apace as you reflect on the remarkable Iowans whose lives we honor."[1]

tical. Ken's consulting for Vermeer continued for three years, well beyond the campaign.

As part of his work, Ken met with Vermeer leaders and provided feedback to Dad. One of Ken's suggestions was to formalize the structure of our board of directors. He also sensed my interest in the business, and he suggested that Dad put me on that board. Dad took Ken's suggestion, and I joined the board in 1975.

Dad's bond with Galen Byker, who was president of Calvin College from 1995 to 2012, included a shared love for hunting. Over the decades, Mom and Dad made multiple trips to Grand Rapids, home to Calvin College and Seminary. Dad flew there for denominational board meetings, as well as to visit children and grandchildren when they attended Calvin College. When my parents made those trips, their carry-on often included a small cooler filled with ice and freshly dressed squirrel—a gift for Gaylen and Susan Byker. Gaylen appeared pleased with their gift; in return, he provided them with grouse from his own hunting adventures. The two men shared an additional bond: Gaylen had had a successful business career in the energy sector before becoming Calvin's president. Dad appreciated his understanding of the business world.

His relationship with William (Bill) Spoelhof, Gaylen's predecessor as Calvin College's president, began while Stan and I attended Calvin and continued when my parents attended Calvin basketball games to watch their granddaughter, Mindi. Bill had retired as college president in 1976, but he remained visible on campus, keeping regular office hours and socializing with faculty and students. He was an enthusiastic basketball fan, attending every home game of both Calvin's men's and women's teams. When Mom and Dad watched Mindi play for the Calvin Knights, they often found Bill sitting at the south end of the gym watching the game. They enjoyed conversations with him at these home games.

Dad respected Bill's college leadership. During his tenure, an entirely new college campus was created. The original campus on Franklin Street was landlocked, so college and church officials purchased Knollcrest Farm, four hundred acres in east Grand Rapids, and built Knollcrest Campus. Leading the college through this significant move positively marked Dr. Spoelhof's presidency. It allowed Calvin College to grow into the future, both from a physical- and a curriculum-based perspective.[2]

Despite Dad's legendary skepticism about higher education, he certainly enjoyed the company of academics! Nevertheless, achieving degrees did not impress Dad. His litmus test remained firm: a person's ability to use that degree in the business and professional world.

RESTLESS CURIOSITY

Sometimes, Dad's restless energy and insatiable curiosity could be draining for those around him. In Canada, when the weather didn't allow us to fly out to our favorite fishing spots, keeping him occupied could be a challenge. He would often walk laps around the camp. Of course he knew exactly how many laps were required for a mile walk. He had counted out the steps, and five times around the camp made a mile. When weather kept us bound to the camp, we would walk enough loops to log several miles. Other times, we boated twenty minutes to the nearest road, then walked a mile or so to Sunset Cafe for lunch.

Although Dad was not consistently interested in reading, for some topics a book could totally absorb his attention.

Once, when just Mom, Dad, and Jason were at the camp, Dad became fascinated by a book on the history of aviation. Jason and Mom were delighted to have free time to do their reading and projects without entertaining Dad or going along on yet another outing.

One topic that continued to interest Dad over a long time period was the Northwest Passage. As Jason once said, "Grandpa had an insatiable curiosity about certain issues, and he was fascinated by the Northwest Passage." Since it was hard to find gifts for Dad, many family members sought out books about the places or historical events that intrigued him. When Jason was in graduate school at MIT in Boston, I searched the Harvard bookstore for a gift and was delighted to find a book on the Northwest Passage, which I gave him as a Christmas gift.

Why the Northwest Passage? Perhaps because it is in the far north and the challenges of the Arctic temperatures consistently fascinated him. Perhaps because of its history: a century of exploration in which sailors repeatedly tried to find a water route in the northern hemisphere between the Atlantic and Pacific Oceans. Perhaps because of the controversy about ownership of that waterway. Or perhaps because he simply became curious about it at some point and then kept encountering more information to add to his storehouse.

Dad's love of the frigid zones went beyond the Northwest Passage. My parents made two trips to Antarctica, one to the North Pole, and multiple trips to Alaska. Long before the idea of a bucket list was popular, Dad enjoyed travel. Seeing new places and learning about them energized him. He was curious about other countries as well as his own.

The first time Dad and Mom traveled to Antarctica, Dad reported he had sat next to an interesting guy named Jim, who told them he wrote books about various places around the world. Dad was fascinated that he had written a book about South Africa. Although Jim had traveled the globe doing research for his books, he had never before been to Antarctica.

As my parents told us more, we realized that the "Jim" Dad was talking about was James Michener, and the book on South Africa was *The Covenant*. Because of Dad's interest in South Africa, that was the one Michener book he had read. As a Michener fan, who had read almost all of his novels, I was jealous. I wished I had been part of that conversation!

TRAVELLING TO THE BIG THREE

People who travel internationally often list the three As as favorite destinations: Alaska, Australia, and Africa. Over the decades, Dad and Mom traveled to all three several times.

The first trip to Alaska was in 1960. Our family of five flew in a single-engine Beechcraft Bonanza from Pella to Regina, Saskatchewan. After a night in Regina, we flew to Dawson Creek, where we started to follow 1,700 miles of the Alaska Highway, constructed during World War II for transporting United States troops to Alaska. Dad wanted to follow that highway by plane through the mountains of Canada. If we had any engine issues, we could always do an emergency landing on the highway.

That was our last family trip in the Bonanza. I was ten, Bob was fifteen, and Stan was seventeen and starting college in the fall. Stan was usually the copilot, while Mom, Bob, and I were sandwiched in the bench seat in back. We were in Alaska on June 21, the longest day of the year. We attended a Fairbanks baseball game that day and marveled at the way it stayed light far into the night. Dad loved unique experiences like that.

My parents made another trip to Alaska in January to see it with little or no daylight. They spent several nights in Point Barrow, Alaska, the northernmost city in the United States, located above the Arctic Circle. In Barrow (population 4,000), my parents attended local basketball games, a mainstay entertainment in many Alaskan towns. At their favorite breakfast café, local residents were eager to talk to them. They were treated like celebrities and were interviewed for the local radio station. Very few tourists went to Barrow in January!

In 1999, Dad and Jason both wanted to fly the Alaska Highway route, with Jason as pilot. Jason asked if he could take his girlfriend, Carrie Anderson, along. Dad said yes. They visited Barrow again, and Jason proposed to Carrie

Gary and Matilda on the Alaska trip in 1999 with Jason and Carrie

on Barrow's beach. After all, they were staying at the Top of the World Hotel, and Jason thought that was a pretty good place to propose. Carrie said yes, and they went to my parents' room to share their news. Jason and Carrie had been dating a year, so Mom and Dad had been anticipating this announcement at some point. They responded with hugs and congratulations.

My parents' last trip to Alaska was in 2006. Dad's health was failing, but it was a trip he wanted to make one last time. This time they drove the Alaska Highway, and Mom was the driver. Their health didn't permit the adventures of previous trips, but they relished the trip down memory lane.

On that same trip, they called home several times to ask, "Has that little girl arrived?" Jason and Carrie were expecting their second child, and we did not know the gender of the baby. But Dad was sure it would be a girl. Mia was born the day they arrived back in Pella. Dad was tickled to hold her—and of course very pleased that his prediction had been right.

Dad loved animals and the outdoors. Locally, he liked seeing squirrels, rabbits, deer, turkey, ducks, and geese, but he also enjoyed watching elk in Montana, admiring lions and elephants in Africa, and searching for moose in Canada. Seated on a swing at Lundy's camp in Canada, he and Mom loved relaxing on a summer evening, watching the sun go down and then listening to the loons.

Dad and Mom were very generous in giving trips to members of their extended family. For their fiftieth anniversary, they took all of their descendants to Africa on safari. When Dad first brought up the idea of our entire family going to Africa on safari, not all of us were immediately

A map of Tanzania, the destination of the Vermeer safari trip

ready to go. We had lots of reasons for why the timing might not work.

Dad responded, "I want to go with the grandkids to show them the game parks. If you kids want to come along, you may." He

The family on safari

was eager to give his grandchildren a wonderful and exciting experience. He wasn't going to be stopped by his children finding reasons not to go.

Both generations cleared their schedules and went to three parks in Tanzania: Ngorongoro Crater, Serengeti, and Lake Manyara. Every evening after dinner, we gathered in one spot in whichever lodge we were staying and our guide,

A giraffe siting in Tanzania

who had worked there for decades, told us stories from the parks' past.

Dad and Mom loved providing these experiences for their family. Dad got excited seeing his children and grandchildren spot a lion resting on a big rock, gaze at fighting giraffes, encounter wild dogs, watch hippos drink at watering holes, and thrill to the beauty of gazelles.

Dad and Mom also toured the third A—Australia—several times. Their favorite trips there included taking a train east from Perth across the continent. Dad thought Perth was one of the prettiest cities in the world. He loved its black swans, the only place he ever saw them. Of course, spotting kangaroos and wallabies also provided highlights.

OTHER TRAVEL LEARNING

In the late 1950s, Cuba provided a new travel experience. Fidel Castro had just overthrown the Batista government.

Gary standing in the ruins of Angkor Wat

In 1959, the Cuban people had suffered under the dictator Batista, and they believed this change in government would be good for their country. In the spring of 1960, Dad and my brother, Stan, made this trip together. They flew the Beechcraft Bonanza to Florida and then took a commercial flight to Cuba. In Cuba, Stan ate his first shrimp cocktail. He said, "I was impressed with a visit to a palace where many of the Batista treasures, such silver items, were for sale." It was the end of an era and the beginning of a regime that would last nearly six decades.

In 1963, my parents made a three-month journey around the world. They visited missionaries, business connections, and one-of-a-kind sites. The sites included Cambodia's Angkor Wat. Covering 402 acres, it is the largest religious monument in the world. Dad was fascinated by the level of vibrant civilization evident in the ruins of the Angkor Wat temple. He took lots of pictures of Angkor Wat. He was impressed with the jungle surrounding the site and the remarkable structure that rose out of that jungle. Whenever Dad listed sites he considered world treasures, Angkor Wat was at the top of the list.

The first Western visitor to the temple was a Portuguese monk, who visited in 1586. He said, "It is of such extraordinary construction that it is not possible to describe it with a pen, particularly since it is like no other building in the world. It has towers and decoration and all the refinements which the human genius can conceive of."[3]

That trip around the world also included India, where they rode elephants and visited the Taj Mahal. A stop in Egypt included tours of the pyramids. King Tut's tomb was of particular interest to Dad. King Tut had been in power from approximately 1332 to 1323 B.C. After his death at age nineteen, he disappeared from history until the discovery of his tomb in 1922. As millions have done since then, Dad marveled at the level of civilization that had been in existence centuries ago.

CURIOSITY AT HOME

Not all of Dad's curiosity questions were asked or answered on long trips. Many were close to home. Dad's younger cousin, Marsha Jansen Overbergen, thought it was special when Dad called her and asked, "Is it okay if Matilda and I drive over to see your grapevines?

Marsha and her husband grew grapes. Dad was interested in seeing the vines and picking a few clusters. Marsha recalled, "It was very interesting that a person like Gary, who could easily buy grapes and certainly didn't need to pick them, enjoyed the experience of grape picking."

Gary and Matilda stop at the Taj Mahal in 1963

Gary and Matilda riding camels in Egypt in 1963

When sour cherries were ripe, Dad wanted to go to Stan's house to pick a few and eat them. Eating them as an adult brought back memories of enjoying them in his youth.

Dad and Mom also enjoyed finding morel mushrooms in the spring. Mom was outstanding at finding them in my parents' or friends' timberland, where they hid under fallen leaves or nested among the roots of trees. After a successful hunt, they enjoyed telephoning family members and inviting them for a lunch of fried morels. Mom rinsed the freshly picked morels in salt water, then sautéed them in a flour-and-cornmeal breading. For my parents, both the finding and the sharing were a pleasure.

Both Dad and Mom enjoyed interacting with their grand-children. They were very intentional about spending time with each of them, whether vacationing in Canada, hunting in Iowa, or attending sporting events, musical concerts, or theatrical productions.

On the Calvin basketball team, Mindi played point guard, a position that required calling the plays. Dad quizzed her after games, especially after close ones. He asked, "How did you know what to do at the end of the game? Did you call the play, or did your coach tell you what to call?" He wanted to know about her decision-making process.

Part of the time Mindi and her husband, Frank, lived in Grand Rapids, Mindi worked at Fifth Third Bank as a treasury account officer. When my parents visited them, Dad asked her questions about the bank: "What are the assets in the bank? What cash do you have? How are fed funds doing?" When Mindi knew that Grandma and Grandpa were coming for a visit, she began checking out answers to the questions that she expected from Grandpa.

Matilda and Gary frequently attended Mindi's college basketball games

A visit to Grand Rapids in the early 2000s with Frank and Mindi

Mom and Dad also thoroughly enjoyed playing cards with their grandkids. Their grandchildren have warm memories of playing Rook or Five-Point Pitch around the kitchen table in Pella or in the cabin in Canada.

Some evenings in Canada, Dad wanted to quit playing cards and go to bed early. My mother desperately wanted to keep him up a little later so perhaps he wouldn't wake all of us at five the next morning. Some evenings, Mom forced him to stay up to play cards. Once he got into the game, even though he had really wanted to go to sleep early, he was extremely competitive. Playing Hearts, he loved to shoot the moon (go for all the points). He didn't mind losing hands as long as a few times he could go for all the points and win.

As with basketball, Dad was particularly interested in the strategy others used in a card game. After a hand, especially if he lost, he would ask his opponent "Why did you lay that card?"

ACTIVE IN LATER YEARS

Dad and Mom enjoyed new adventures at every age—well into their eighties. In the late 1990s, each of their three children arranged and paid for a special trip with them. Dale and I arranged a winter trip to a high-altitude ranch in Wyoming. We flew into Jackson Hole, where we made a stop to see a herd of elk. From there we drove north to Brooks Lake Lodge, which was owned by a good friend. The lodge was located at an altitude of 11,000 feet and surrounded by the Teton Mountains. We took snowmobiles to the lodge and then enjoyed ice fishing, snowshoeing, and—the highlight—dogsledding.

Brooks Lake Lodge, 1999

Mom wanted to be the musher. Mushers need to control the dogs totally by voice, and even at age seventy-nine Mom was up for the challenge. On one corner, though, she was thrown off the sled and landed in the snow. She got right up and was ready to get back into musher position. And Dad and Mom enjoyed snowmobiling so much that in subsequent winters they went to Yellowstone National Park, rented snowmobiles, and toured the park grounds.

Denise Park, psychological scientist and lead researcher of the University of Texas, said, "It is important to get out and do something that is unfamiliar and mentally challenging and that provides broad stimulation mentally and socially. When you are inside your comfort zone, you may be outside of the enhancement zone."[4]

As long as my parents were physically able to, they entered the enhancement zone. They continued to try new adventures, learn interesting facts, and share many of these experiences with family and friends. They were excellent models for how to make the most of every day, no matter what their age.

Gary and Matilda on a train trip in Canada

REMEMBERING PLEASURE FROM A HOSPICE BED

During Dad's final days, when he was under hospice care, I visited him after I had just arrived back from a meeting in California, where I had seen Catalina Island from the California coast. In previous years, when Jason and Carrie lived in Pasadena, Dad had been thrilled when Jason flew him from the El Monte airport to Catalina, known as the "Airport in the Sky." It sits atop a mountain—actually atop two mountains. In 1946, the canyon between two peaks was filled to create a 3,200-foot runway. Jason and Dad landed above the clouds, enjoyed a buffalo burger at the airport café, and then returned.

Sitting next to Dad's bed, I mentioned how much we had enjoyed flying to Catalina with Jason and landing on a mountaintop. Dad smiled and said, "That's a favorite memory for me, too." Now, whenever we are along the Pacific Ocean in California, I look into the distance, trying to spot Catalina. When I see it, I think of Dad and his joy flying to the Airport in the Clouds.

4 | Heart of an Entrepreneur

Tinkering, Project Planning, and Intuition

One quality many entrepreneurs have in common is their ability to see a need and act on it. Dad demonstrated that quality as he worked on his father's farm.

TINKERING WITH FARM EQUIPMENT

When he worked with his father, Dad liked to tinker in the farm's shop, which was heated during winter by a corncob stove. A piece of that shop is preserved in the Vermeer Museum, along with one of my favorite photos. It is from 1939, and Dad is standing near a John Deere tractor with a cab. Looking at that photo with Dad, I once asked him, "Did other people have cabs on their tractors in 1939?"

"Back then, nobody had cabs on tractors," he answered.

Dad had created that one-of-a-kind cab in the Vermeer farm workshop. According to a 1939 *Pella Chronicle* article, Dad built the cab from sheet metal, car glass, and ceiling lumber. The photo caption noted:

> *Riding a tractor in the open and dragging a disk on Thursday April 6th was a bitter cold job for the wind was due north and it searched out the ears, the fingers, and the shoe tops and curled up the back. Most of the farmers sowing oats and disking that day had faces the color of a ripe Jonathan apple. But Gary Vermeer, who lives two miles east, rode in comfort.*[1]

The 1939 cab designed by Gary for his John Deere tractor. Photo from The Pella Chronicle, *April 20, 1939.*

Later, Uncle John told me more details. "Before we had that cab, we used to put the front wheel of the tractor into the furrow and then jump off the seat and walk alongside the tractor," he explained. "If the tractor went off track or we needed to turn a corner, we quickly jumped back on. It wasn't very safe, but it was so cold sitting on the tractor during cold days that we would rather jump off and on. During cold weather, that cab made our work a lot warmer."

Although a tractor cab never became part of the Vermeer business product offerings, it certainly improved Dad's working conditions on the family farm.

During World War II, when farmers still picked corn by hand, Dad and his father asked the war-rationing board for permission to purchase a two-row mechanical corn picker for their farm. The board granted permission, but because many of the men from the area were part of the war effort, the board required that Dad and his father also use the picker to help other farmers harvest corn.

Harvesting for multiple farmers required efficiency, and scooping corn from wagons was time consuming. So Dad created a time-saver: a simple hoist that elevated the front end of the wagon, making it easy to scoop corn from the back end.

Neighboring farmers who saw his invention asked him to make a similar hoist for them. First, Dad went to a local blacksmith shop; the results were not what he wanted. In that moment, Vermeer Manufacturing was conceived. In 1948, at age thirty, Dad decided to start his own manufacturing company.

He mentioned the decision to his father, who skeptically replied, "I don't think you can make any money doing that."

Over the decades, Dad enjoyed telling people about this conversation. He would often quote his father's opinion that there was no money to be made in manufacturing and pause for dramatic effect.

Then he would grin and say in a classic understatement, "He was wrong."

Grandpa Vermeer had good reason to prefer farming over manufacturing. The years after World War II were profitable ones for most farmers. Stan remembers Dad saying, "If you couldn't make money farming after World War II, then you shouldn't have been farming."

By the time Dad started Vermeer Manufacturing, he already had been successfully farming since he graduated from high school. First, he farmed with this father. Then when my parents married in 1941, Grandpa Vermeer gave

Buerkens Wagons

Uncle John Vermeer, Dad's younger brother, remembers using Buerkens wagons on their family farm. Since the Buerkens wagons had been manufactured in Pella for decades, many of those first wagon hoists were used with Buerkens wagons.

Buerkens wagons were named after their manufacturer, Barney Buerkens, a Pella resident who had previously made buggies and wagons in the Netherlands. According to the Historic Pella Trust:

> *It had a lot of specialized machinery and was a lot of fun to watch operate...They had machines that cut the spokes of the wheels at their correct length and made the ferrules for the wheels on a particular machine...The Beurkens Wagon Factory became very well known all over the state.*[2]

Production of Buerkens wagons ended in 1957 when a fire demolished the building in which the wagons were manufactured.

The first product produced by Vermeer Manufacturing was the wagon hoist, used with a Buerkens wagon.

them a 120-acre farm a quarter mile east and a quarter mile north of the homestead, with the understanding that they would gradually pay him for it as their farm income permitted. So, although they had no bank debt on their farm, they did owe money to Dad's parents.

TAKING A RISK

According to the dictionary, an entrepreneur is "a person who organizes and manages any enterprise, especially a business, usually with considerable initiative and risk."[3] Entrepreneurs often have to be willing to risk lack of income and uncertainty from day to day.

Part of Dad's risk in the first years of Vermeer Manufacturing was his use of an inheritance of $12,000 from an uncle and aunt who had been close to him, Art and Bertha Van Donselaar. It was, however, the moderate risk typical of entrepreneurs. He and Mom could live on their farm income, so he was probably comfortable investing that inheritance money in the new business.

Dad took no salary from the company in its first ten years. Instead, my parents lived frugally on their farm income. Mom had grown up with very little money, so she was well equipped to make do with what she had. She didn't waste. Often, we saw her wipe down aluminum foil to reuse or rinse out plastic bags to use again.

Art and Bertha Van Donselaar

FARMING WITH INTUITION

"You cannot ignore your intuition," Bill Gates, a penultimate entrepreneur, once said.[4]

The dictionary definition for intuition is "the ability to understand something immediately, without the need for conscious reasoning."[5] Often in life, there is no clear evidence one way or the other, and a judgement must be made based on intuition. Although Dad definitely was a man who reasoned, he based many decisions on his good intuition.

As a farmer, Dad had some very tight guidelines, likely based on intuition. Each season, he followed specific processes for planting corn and beans. He was adamant that he would not start planting until April 15, even though

Entrepreneur Dealers Followed Dad's Model

As many of Vermeer's industrial dealers started their own entrepreneurial ventures with Vermeer, they also risked personal comfort in order to get their enterprise into a secure financial state. The ones who did well in their business often lived frugally in order to make payroll for their employees and pay for the whole goods and parts they received from Vermeer.

Among those early dealer couples were Junior and Bev Kool. Junior started working for Vermeer in the factory in-weld cleanup. He met Dad when he was asked to work with him on a project on the farm. While they worked, Junior mentioned he would probably quit working at Vermeer and go into business with his brother.

Dad asked, "Why would you do that?"

Junior answered, "I just like to work outside, and working with my brother would let me do that."

Dad suggested that he might be interested in switching to working in sales for Vermeer. And soon, Junior and his wife were asked if they would be willing to run a dealership in California. As parents of three young children,

I think he was itching to start sooner when we had an early spring. As family members, we knew if we wanted Dad at a Charitable Foundation meeting—or any other meeting—we needed to schedule it before April 15. In the fall, we waited to schedule events until November, after harvest had been completed. Despite the growing business, farming remained Dad's number-one priority.

According to Uncle John, he and Dad had plowed the fields during every month of the year. Iowa weather is, after all, unpredictable. Reflecting on Dad's April 15 planting date, John recalled that in the early farming decades he and Dad didn't start planting until May. In later years, hybrid development allowed them to start earlier than April 15.

it was a huge step for them, but they said yes—for just a one-year time period. In 1965, when they returned to Pella, Junior said that someday he would like to own a dealership.

For the next six years, he worked as a factory representative with dealers and sales people around the country. In 1971, he was asked if he wanted to buy a dealership in Eureka, Illinois. He said yes. To help finance this venture, Junior sold his part of a farm he owned with this brother. Two Vermeer team members also loaned him capital. Running that dealership was a family affair. Bev worked in the office during the children's school hours. When they were old enough, all three children worked at the dealership after school. The Kools paid back those loans in three years. They are just one example of the entrepreneurial spirit evident among Vermeer industrial and agricultural dealers.

Today, we still see new dealers who sacrifice comforts and stability in their lives to establish a solid dealership. They are true entrepreneurs, and we are proud to work with them.

Dad always planted corn first, and then he planted beans in May. When the spring was rainy, Dad stayed calm about getting his crop in. In those years, he talked about how late you could plant and still get a good crop. Because of his experience and intuition, he didn't worry about the weather. Once the company was established, he had an alternative income and the risk posed by weather did not loom as large for him as it did for other farmers.

For many years, Dad and my brother, Bob, owned farms together. Dad usually made the decisions about when to sell the crop. Bob recalled, "He held on to the crop until the summer, selling it usually about nine months after harvest. And he never wanted to buy crop insurance on the farms." Bob also recalled that when the two of them made a profit on a farm, the money stayed in the bank. When they had accumulated a certain amount and could pay cash for a farm that came on the market, they added to their farm acres and bought more land.

Dad also used his sense of market trends at Vermeer. For example, John Vander Wert remembers that Dad had an accurate intuition about coming economic downturns. About a half year before each downturn of the early 1960s, 1970s, and 1980s, Dad told the company team members to start reducing purchases and finished inventory. "You'd better slow down," he would warn them. Dad was somewhat lenient on purchased-items inventory, but he did not like finished goods sitting around. Inventory meant cash was sitting in the machines and reducing liquidity for the business.

During his entire life, no matter how much the company grew, Dad remained a farmer at heart. He continued to work on his farms into his late eighties. When he eventually found it difficult to climb up into the tractor, he decided it was time to sell the farm machinery. It was a sad day for him and for his family because we all knew how much he loved planting each spring and harvesting each fall.

PLEASURE IN PROJECTS

Dad loved having projects both on the farm and at the company. In 1968, Dad and Mom started spending much of each summer in Canada—and those summers offered forty years of new project opportunities.

In 1968, the summer after my high school graduation, I traveled with my parents to Dave's Wilderness Camp in Ontario, Canada. At that time, the camp was owned by John and Vi Vande Noord, a couple from Pella. It was on the banks of Wabaskang Lake. Its address was Perrault Falls, but the only available form of transportation from Perrault Falls to the camp was a boat. The camp passed through the hands of several owners until it was purchased by Jerry and Sally Lundy, who became good friends of Dad and Mom during their final years of spending the summer in Canada.

Dad enjoyed helping with camp projects. When we first vacationed there, the cabins had no indoor plumbing. Over the years, improvements were made, but the camp retained its Canadian wilderness charm. All of the Vermeer clan enjoyed time at the camp with Dad and Mom. Eventually, Dad created a spring tradition. He talked with each of his children, asking when we would like to go with them to Canada. Then he jotted the dates in a small notebook he always carried in his shirt pocket. As the grandchildren reached elementary-school ages, Dad and Mom often took the grandkids with them in small groups, without their parents—outings the grandchildren now recall fondly.

One of the vacations when the whole family gathered in Canada during the same week

For many years, each time my parents took family or friends to the camp they left some of their tackle, shore lunch, and cooking supplies in the cabin. They boxed these items and stored them until their next return trip. After the first season of Lundy ownership, Dad asked, "Can you assure me that next summer we will be able to have Cabin Four?" Cabin Four was the newest structure at the camp, with a nice kitchen and an indoor bathroom.

To Dad's disappointment, Jerry replied, "Sorry, Gary. I can't do that because other guests have already reserved that cabin for the next season."

Dad, in problem-solving mode, then asked, "Could you build a cabin for me?"

Jerry said he had no time to build a cabin.

Dad thought a moment and said, "What if I build the cabin and make a rental payment for the next five years?"

Jerry said he would think it over. When he left for Iowa, Dad had no commitment from Jerry.

The next time he arrived in Canada, though, he smiled as he walked up the hill from the dock and saw an area roped off in preparation for a new cabin. Jerry and Dad immediately had a conversation about building specifics. Dad had the amount for the rental fee in mind, and he had a drawing of the cabin he wanted. Then, to Jerry's amazement, Dad said he would also pay to upgrade Jerry's generator. Dad had thought ahead and realized that that an additional cabin would strain the capacity of the current generator.

They came to an agreement. Jerry remembers, "At that point, Gary looked like a five-year-old at Christmas!"

Dad was pleased with having a new designated cabin for his family. In addition, it provided him with another project, which soon became a family project. My brother, Stan, custom crafted the cabinets. My son, Jason, also helped with the project when he had free hours between flying guests out to fish at different lakes. Mom was especially grateful. She could leave items in Canada for the entire season. She no longer had to totally pack and unpack for every visit.

Jason was Dad's bush pilot for five years, and he also recalls that his grandpa loved doing projects at the camp. Participating in those projects with his grandfather—whether it was building a cabin or fixing a fishing boat motor or the dock at Sharp Lake—was a major reason Jason studied engineering in college.

Jerry was amazed at how much Dad observed and remembered when he was at the camp. Early one morning, after a very stormy night, he noticed that the wind had blown against the seaplane, which was tied to the dock. The force of the wind on the airplane's tail had caused the dock to start pulling away from the shore. By 5:00 a.m., Dad was at Jerry's door. Jerry was usually up and having coffee outside at 5:00 a.m., but since it had been stormy he was still in the cabin. Dad said he an idea of what they should do to stabilize the dock and prevent it from breaking in the future.

He told Jerry the details, "We need to have an 800-pound weight to stabilize the dock. There's enough gravel on another part of your property. We can use that…we will need some cement." Jerry boated into Perrault Falls and returned with cement. They created a form and poured in the concrete mix and gravel. They had their 800-pound anchor!

Dad had also noticed some long poles, and he knew Jerry had a power winch on the property. With a couple of strong young men to help, they brought the concrete form to the edge of the water, where they maneuvered it onto the two poles. Because the anchor weighed less once it was in the water, it could be moved to the correct area to properly anchor the dock.

Jason recalled that Jerry was uncertain if Dad's ideas for maneuvering the large concrete block would work, but they did it. Jerry said the anchor continued to work well for the remaining years he owned the camp. Jason remembers that he thought, *If Grandpa has tried something like this before and it worked, he is totally confident in his suggestions.*

Dad had also noticed an engine block to one side of the generator house. The engine block was not being used, so Dad asked Jerry if he could use it as an anchor in the nearby cove so he could keep the seaplane in the cove overnight whenever a storm was expected. As soon as Dad had noticed the unused engine block, he knew he needed an alternative

The cabin Gary built

Gary and Matilda preparing fresh fish in their cabin at Lundy's Wilderness Camp

place for the seaplane…and he loved a project! Jerry said Dad was always observing, always taking in what was around him and using that knowledge as he solved problems.

INTUITION ABOUT PEOPLE

Dad was not only observing the camp, though. He was also observing the Lundys. After three years of getting to know Jerry and Sally, Dad asked Jerry to stop in Pella on his fall return trip from the camp to Dowagiac, Michigan. When Jerry arrived at Vermeer Corporate headquarters, Dad met Jerry in his office and asked, "Jerry, what do you owe on the camp?"

When Jerry told him the amount, Dad got out his checkbook and wrote a check for that amount. He asked Jerry to pay him back in five years, and they shook hands. Jerry was pleased that he could pay off that loan in just one and one half years.

But for me, the real story is that Dad had been observing and interacting with the Lundys for over three years. He liked their work ethic and gracious hospitality, and he wanted them to succeed. Dad knew that it was not easy to make a profit on a camp. Needing to transport everything by boat created high overhead costs. Jerry said that with that loan he realized Dad had been evaluating him and Sally, leading Jerry to develop great respect for Dad's ability to evaluate people.

Entrepreneurs need to evaluate people who want to be part of their business. In the early days of Vermeer, we didn't have a formal hiring process or a Human Resources Department. If people were looking for a job, acquaintances advised them to go to Vermeer on Saturday morning. Dad was in the office on Saturday and might hire you on the spot. The word was that Dad asked just a couple questions of anyone looking for a job. The first question was, "Who are your folks?" If he knew an applicant's parents, he had an idea of the work ethic of the person looking for a job. He also asked, "Do you milk cows?" If the person came from a farm and milked cows, they could be relied upon. Milking cows meant you were up early and had to be responsible in your duties. These questions gave Dad a sense of whether the person asking for a job would be a good fit at Vermeer.

The principle behind Dad's question about milking cows is still relevant in today's job market. Finding a skilled workforce is a big issue for employers; one of the most important sets of skills a potential employee should have are the soft skills—showing up every day for work and completing tasks. Dad's question about milking cows helped him get at whether a person had those soft skills.

Dad also took advantage of individual time with team members to not only to get to know them better, but to understand what future roles they might be interested in. Sometimes those conversations happened while working on a project on the farm. Other times, they happened while flying. If Dad needed to go somewhere in Iowa and there was a convenient airport, he would fly himself to the destination. He often invited someone to fly along. John Vander Wert recalls flying along with Dad in the plane to Marshalltown to meet with a vendor when he was new to the company. John had a connection with Dad because his father had been Matilda's country school teacher. On the flight back from Marshalltown, Dad asked John, "What are your goals?"

John answered, "I would like to earn $10,000 a year." At that time, his salary was around $6,000.

Dad thought that might be possible. Then he asked, "What job do you want to get?"

John answered, "Your job."

Dad said that might not be possible. Then he asked his last question. "Who do you admire at Vermeer?"

John first answered, "Harry," but Dad asked him to exclude owners from his choices.

So John said, "Arnie Mathes."

Dad liked that answer. He commented, "You know, Arnie doesn't always agree with me, and that is good." John took Dad's comment as advice that he should also be willing to speak his mind when he didn't agree with Dad.

At John Vander Wert's retirement celebration, Dad made a statement that John really appreciated: "There are two kinds of people—people who do less than you think they would or people who do more than you think they would. John, you were one of the latter." Dad did have intuition about people. In the case of John and many others, he definitely chose the right team members—people who helped him grow the business.

Dad was truly an entrepreneur with intuition.

Many happy evenings were spent at Lundy's Wilderness Camp.

5 | Communication

The Value of Being Clear, Concise, and to the Point

Dad modeled a very succinct speaking style. He focused on his point, using a few key stories. I don't think he was ever accused of speaking too long or of boring his audience. From him, I learned that getting to the point is usually a good way to approach a presentation.

When I was in grade school, Dad sometimes preached at rural churches in the Pella area, such as Lower Grove Church near New Sharon. I don't remember seeing him prepare for those sermons—and at that age I was incapable of evaluating his preaching skills—but his openness to serving in a variety of ways is a lesson that has remained with me.

LEARNING FROM HIS MODEL

As a child, I saw Dad prepare at home for speeches to employees, dealers, and customers. He usually picked up a ballpoint pen and a couple of three-by-five note cards, then walked down the short hallway to the master bedroom. Our ranch-style home, built in 1953, was very comfortable but not large. We certainly didn't have a separate room for him to use as an office or study. My parents' bedroom, measuring ten feet by fourteen feet, had just enough space for a queen bed, a dresser, and one chair.

After ten or fifteen minutes in the bedroom, Dad would open the door and come back through the hall. He was prepared for his speech. There were just a few words on the cards—prompts for stories or specific comments. He had a repertoire of stories, and he only needed a word or two to remind him of one. A card with a few notes fit this style perfectly.

Dad probably didn't consider himself my speech coach, but he did fill that role. When I was in fourth grade, I mentioned at the kitchen table during dinner that I was nervous about reading in front of class the next day.

Dad asked me, "Would you be nervous if you were reading to a field of cabbage?"

I smiled. "Of course not!"

"Well," he said, "just imagine that you are talking in front of a roomful of cabbages." He was very matter-of-fact and very practical, providing imagery to help me through the situation. His straightforward advice and tone also told me he had confidence in me; I would do just fine.

I did picture my classmates as cabbages that day, and I made it through that reading—and many speeches and readings after that. That conversation with Dad is still as clear to me as if it happened yesterday.

At the end of my eighth-grade year, I was selected to be class speaker for graduation. I carefully wrote my speech, which was several pages long. During our rehearsal at Pella's First Christian Reformed Church on graduation morning, I read my speech with my written script in front of me. My principal, who was at the practice, suggested that it would be great if I did the speech without notes. Being extremely naïve—and also overly confident—I walked up to the stage that evening with no notes. I got through only the first two lines. Then I totally blanked out. My eighth-grade home room teacher, Mrs. Evie Stravers was seated

Me with my freshman year debate partner, Linda De Jong. Photo from our Pella Christian High School yearbook.

in the third row of pews and had my script on her lap. She could see I was in trouble, so she called out the beginning of the next line.

I have very little memory of the rest of that speech—except that I thanked all the parents multiple times. Recently, I asked two classmates if they remembered my speech fiasco. One of them did not remember. The other remembers I had been upset about it after the ceremony. When it was time for the class picture, she came to get me from where I was hiding out in the church basement.

Her version of the event, after more than four decades, is this: "You had a great speech. We eighth graders all heard it earlier that day, and we all knew you had worthwhile things to say."

She said she wouldn't have remembered anything about the speech except that she was sent down to get me because I had stayed in the basement feeling bad. Her strongest memory of the event? "There were metal strips on the edge of each step. As I ran down the steps, I caught one of my new heels on the last strip and fell. All I could think was, 'What a klutz!' And somebody had seen me fall!"

As self-conscious adolescents, we both had a fiasco that night. Yet both of us managed to smile and look happy for that picture. And we both have the photo to prove it!

After the photo session, Dad went looking for me, knowing I was upset about my speech. He said to me—again in his matter-of-fact voice—that he had found it was better not to memorize his speeches.

He said, "It is better to just have a few notes with you when you speak and use those notes to remember the content you want to share." Painful though it was, that was one of the best speech lessons I learned from Dad.

As a freshman at Pella Christian High School, I decided to join the Debate Club. I knew my dad had enjoyed debate when he was in high school. I thought it would be a good way for me to do something he liked and improve my speaking ability. The topic for the 1964–1965 school year was "Resolved: That nuclear weapons should be controlled by an international organization." This was a timely topic since these were the Cold War years and many people were building shelters in preparation for a nuclear war. I was the first affirmative speaker for our team, and therefore also first for rebuttal. My friend, Linda De Jong, was my debate partner and the second speaker.

As the first speaker, I laid out the basis of our argument on the topic. Then, after all the first speeches on the subject had been made, we had to rebut issues raised by the opposing team. Since Dad had been in debate, he had a few helpful tips. He suggested I prepare various points for the rebuttals so I could make polished responses. I took his advice and prepared responses to what I anticipated would be the arguments made by our opponents.

After my freshman year, I switched to participating in school musical activities and plays. I played Anne Frank's sister, Margot, in *The Diary of Anne Frank,* along with the lead female roles in Gilbert and Sullivan's *HMS Pinafore* and *Pirates of Penzance.*

Dad's lifelong love of theater was sparked when he was in high school. As a member of his church youth group, he acted in their theatrical productions. He also performed in a Pella Community High School production of *The Eagle Screams.*[1] I knew Dad greatly enjoyed attending musicals and plays, so my participation in these was a win for both of us.

Throughout their lives, Dad and Mom continued to enjoy theatrical productions of all sorts—local productions at the high schools and Central College, as well as professional performances at Old Creamery Theatre near the Amana colonies. Theatrical interest has continued in each generation of Vermeers. I smile now when I think how much Dad would have enjoyed being in the audience when his great-grandchildren appeared on stage.

My early experiences of public speaking and performing were a good base for the opportunities I have had to speak publicly—at Vermeer Corporation and beyond.

FROM CLASSROOM TO COMPANY

My years as an elementary teacher added an educator's dimension to my speaking experience. While Dale was finishing at Calvin College, I taught in a second-grade class-room in Grand Rapids, Michigan. Once Dale was notified that he was accepted into the University of Iowa Medical School, we got out an atlas, took a compass, placed the pointed center on Iowa City, and drew the radius of fifty miles. I then wrote sixty-five letters—one for each of the school districts in that fifty-mile radius. After sending out all those letters, I got interviews for jobs in several districts. Because of the music education training I had received at Calvin College, I was given a contract to teach music to first graders at Mark Twain Elementary School and to kindergarten through sixth grade at Hills Elementary school, both of which were in the Iowa City Public School District. Many spouses of medical students were unable to find a local teaching job, so landing a position was a personal victory. Using the thorough and systematic approach to communication Dad had modeled for me paid off!

I taught at both schools daily, starting out with the first-grade classes at Mark Twain in Iowa City and then driving south to Hills and teaching the music to multiple grade levels. After I had taught music for just one year, a kindergarten position became available at the Hills School, and I filled that role instead—continuing to improve my teaching skills.

When I took a leadership role at Vermeer, people some-times asked me how a kindergarten teacher makes the transition to president of a manufacturing company. I told them that the skills sets overlapped. A kindergarten teacher needs to plan, communicate, and motivate; leading a company requires the same skills. When I taught, I was constantly challenged by how to use words that really motivated the children. I was a big believer in using positive reinforcement with each student in the class to get them engaged. So knowing how to communicate and use stories and words to

Mary Kramer: A Teaching Mentor

Mary Kramer, who also taught music at Mark Twain Elementary School, was a teaching mentor for me. I had the privilege of teaching four first-grade classrooms at Mark Twain Elementary School. Mary was the music teacher for the rest of the grades.

Mary often invited several elementary school music teachers to her home to work on ideas and music for classroom use. Typical of teachers in the seventies, we sat in a circle in her living room, playing songs on our guitars like "Dead Skunk in the Middle of the Road." This song, featuring roadkill gore and skunk odors, was useful for piquing interest in music amongst fifth and sixth graders and for teaching them rhythm.

After teaching in Iowa City, Mary went on to become an executive at Wellmark Blue Cross Blue Shield. At Wellmark, Bob Ray, who had just been Governor of Iowa and was CEO of Wellmark, encouraged Mary to run for public office. She ran for the Iowa State Senate, won, and became the first female president of the Iowa Senate. Later, she was appointed as a United States ambassador to Barbados and several Caribbean Islands.

Mary was not only a teaching mentor for me, but also a model for taking responsibilities in corporate and civic life.

positively motivate became part of the tool set that has been useful in my Vermeer career.

Besides, I had heard Dad speak to employees and dealership personnel when I was growing up. He had a motivational communication style that engaged his listeners. When I taught students and when I led a company, I followed in his footsteps.

For example, one of my first job assignments at Vermeer was to teach communication essentials to several classes of plant managers. By leading those classes, I learned a lot about communication as I prepared, and I also learned a lot about the people who are part of the Vermeer organization. The need to communicate skillfully continued as I led sales, dealer, and employee meetings. I enjoy these opportunities; they are an extension of my love of teaching. Dad enjoyed speaking opportunities, too. His favorite audiences were customer groups. He especially enjoyed sharing the story of how the company started and grew.

As the chief operating officer and then the chief executive officer of a mid-size company, I have been able to serve in various capacities in public service. The Iowa Association of Business and Industry asked me to serve as its chair in the early 1990s. Other roles have included chairing the National Association of Manufacturers in 2011–2012, being part of the President's Export Council from 2008 to 2016, and co-chairing the international group of business leaders in the B20. I believe I was selected partly because I have learned to make points that resonate with the audience.

I continue to consider my audience when asked to speak, and I think how a message can best be constructed to be effective for that audience. I don't use a totally scripted speech. I like to have good background on the subject, then think through how I can make points that will resonate. Many of these communication basics go back to what I learned observing Dad—know your audience, know what resonates with them, make your key points, and use stories to reinforce those points.

MOVING TOWARD MORE OPEN COMMUNICATION

In the bigger picture of communication, Dad was very supportive of giving regular feedback to our employees. He believed that giving updates to our team members, in good times and in tough times, was a great way to let our team know we cared about them.

Through the years I worked at the company, from 1982 onward, employee meetings were part of a regular routine for my brothers and for me. In those first years, I walked from plant to plant, often standing outside on the grass in front of a plant with a small microphone to provide team members with a business update.

In the late 1990s, when we began implementing lean processes, we needed to change our manufacturing system from batch fabrication to one-piece flow. We were changing our culture and needed buy-in from Vermeer team members.

In the early years, we had been very private about our sales numbers and our profits. We only informed team members whether sales and profits were expanding or shrinking. As we entered the lean journey, we read studies about the positive results of open-book management. We learned that seeing the financial picture in detail provides important motivation and understanding for all team members.

In the 1980s, we had started learning about open communication from Herman Miller CEO Max De Pree. Max was known for his efforts to combine a caring organization with business success. He often advised us, "Err on the side of over-communication." We learned from him the importance of being authentic, helping our team to understand the reality of economic situations.

As we started our lean journey, we opened up our communication about finances, sharing the dollar amounts of our sales and its percentage of net operating income. Although Dad didn't really give his blessing to this new level of communication, he didn't put up barriers to it either. We

Max De Pree: A Business Mentor

Like me, Max De Pree (1924–2017) was the second-generation leader of a family manufacturing business. Max and his brother, Hugh, assumed leadership of the office furniture manufacturing company Herman Miller in the early 1960s. My brothers and I traveled to Herman Miller in the early 1980s to benchmark what that company was doing with Scanlon, a cost-sharing productivity program. We also wanted to understand Max's thoughts about "covenantal relationships" in the corporate world. As a Calvinist Christian, Max had thought deeply about how to integrate his faith into his work.

That first visit was the beginning of Max's unofficial mentorship.

Max is widely quoted on the responsibilities of leadership, and his book Leadership Is an Art is considered a classic. Max was frequently quoted as saying, "The first responsibility of a leader is to define reality. The last is to say thank you. In between the two, the leader must become a servant and a debtor. That sums up the progress of an artful leader."

I have depended on his ideas, especially in tough times when our team has needed to know that status of reality. I continue to aspire to follow Max's model of servant leadership.

have used different kinds of charts to share these numbers to show the Vermeer story, and we have found that the most effective charts are ones that are simple and easy to read. Lots of data and busy charts can obscure the message. We keep it simple, a principle very much aligned with Dad's philosophy of management.

In one very rough economic time, I got a gigantic version of a dollar bill and cut it up to show how much of each dollar went to purchased items and steel, wages, health care, engineering, finance, IT, sales, service, electricity, etc. That left a very tiny slice—or no slice at all—of the bill for profit. Often, visuals help people better understand both the financial environment and how they could help to improve profitability.

I have learned that clear, concise communication with the team on a regular basis adds value for most team members. New employees often remark that past employers did not take time to share what is happening in the company and that the regular communication is appreciated.

Like Max De Pree, we have realized that we rarely communicate too much. Communicating the same message repeatedly, until the speaker is sick of it, still may not be enough. It is important to repeat the message with new and engaging stories because it takes multiple messages to truly engage a team.

A leader's communication skills may be their most important asset, especially if the communication is authentic—in fact, maybe only if it is authentic.

Once, Max De Pree and I both participated in a conference on faith and work. After I had concluded a presentation and sat down, Max turned to me and asked, "Are you having fun in your career?"

I was astonished because Dad had recently asked me the identical question. Both of them wanted to know if I was passionate about my work and if it gave me fulfillment.

My answer was yes. And I have since asked that question when talking with Vermeer team members. We need to consider, perhaps on a daily basis, if our passions are a match for what we are doing each day. Then we can be authentic. Then we can truly communicate.

6 | Tools for Success

Motivators, Marketing, and Focus

Dad's love for theater, combined with his marketing intuition, served him well in his early adult life. In the late 1940s, when Dad was approaching thirty, he became a leader of the youth group at First Christian Reformed Church. Dad's cousin, Marsha, recalled performing in a church play Dad directed that was staged at the Pella High School auditorium. Marsha remembers Dad being a good director. She once told me, "Everything Gary did, he did well."

Gary's senior class picture, 1935

A KEYCHAIN LEADER FOR YOUTH

When my parents became charter members of Calvary Christian Reformed Church, Dad became a youth leader at that congregation as well and offered to use his directing skills again. The youth group produced *Hans Brinker* in 1955 and *A Man Called Peter* in 1956, using these plays as fundraisers.

An early play produced by the Calvary CRC youth group

Bob Dieleman, a member of that youth group in the late 1950s, remembers it was a vibrant bunch of students—and, with fifty members, one of the largest youth groups in Pella. Several youth from other churches also chose to be part of Calvary's youth group.

The Wednesday night meetings lasted two hours. The first hour was a Bible study, and the second hour was a discussion of current issues. Dad liked to promote discussion on current topics on which there was a range of opinions.

In the fall of 1960, during the Nixon and Kennedy presidential campaigns, Dad thought it would be educational to have three sessions focused on the political process. The youth would have political debates on the issues talked about in the campaign. Most of Pella voted Republican, so Dad selected two of the young men to represent the Democratic viewpoint. Bob was one of them, and he said he appreciated those debate sessions.

Jerry Kloostra was also part of that youth group. He said Dad thrived on discussion at the meetings. At the beginning of a session, Dad would always say, "Let's discuss…" Often, he advised the group, "Study the lesson. We will want to discuss every aspect of it." Sometimes, to promote freer discussion, he divided the group. Each sub-group was told to come up with a number of points related to the lesson for the large group to discuss. Dad made a contest out of the process; the winning group was the one who came up with the most questions.

Jerry had a long-term association with Dad and the youth group. He began as a member of Dad's group at First Christian Reformed Church. As a fellow charter member of Calvary Christian Reformed Church, he joined that youth group. He and his wife, Jan, continued to participate in the group after their marriage.

Dad was a youth leader from the time I was in preschool through my junior high years. On Wednesday evenings, our whole family went to church for an educational night. After my class was over, I would go to find Dad. I sometimes had to wait for him while he stayed after the youth session ended, talking with a few of adolescents from the group. Sometimes they continued discussing the topic; at other times, the conversation shifted to personal issues. Dad was willing to talk about whatever a teen wanted to discuss. He was, I think, a safe adult for them. Jerry said he and the others were able to share very personal issues or questions with Dad, and they trusted him to keep these confidential. Dad both listened and helped them to work through their problems. Jerry recalled, "Gary was a mentor to me—like a dad."

Dad did more than just teach the youth group classes and direct plays. He also provided outings that were opportunities for the youth group to have fun together. In the late 1950s, Dad purchased a recreational area a few miles north of Pella, which we fondly called "the camp." Originally bought as a place to hunt ducks and geese, it quickly became a year-round recreation spot. During the summer, scores of people learned to water ski on its small, half-mile-long pond. If the winter weather permitted, the pond became an outdoor ice skating rink. Dad even put up lights so people could skate at night.

Bob remembers youth group events at the camp—ice skating in the winters, water skiing and volleyball in the summers. Jerry recalled Dad constantly organizing other events, too—snow sledding, wild game dinners, fox hunts, and watermelon hunts. It was no coincidence that these choices coincided with some of Dad's favorite activities.

The plays Dad directed and produced weren't just one-time performances in a single venue. Several of them were performed multiple times in surrounding communities. Some years, the entire troupe traveled to Northwest Iowa and performed on the gym stage at Western Christian High School in Hull.

One of the plays was *Cheaper by the Dozen*. Jerry especially remembers that play in connection with Dad's advice: "Keep the play going." If someone forgot a line, Dad told the other cast members to ad-lib until they got the play back on track. Jerry remembers that at the end of one scene, his script called for reading multiplication tables to the children in the play. The curtain was supposed to close as he was reading. But the person in charge of closing the curtain wasn't paying attention and failed to close them. Jerry told me he just kept rattling off numbers, following Dad's advice. The curtain finally did close, but for Jerry it had been an extremely long few minutes of repeating multiplication tables!

One of the plays that went on the road was *Calamity Kids.* Bob Dieleman, cast as one of the adult men in the play, told me they performed that play three times at the Pella Christian High School gym to sellout crowds, one time in Oskaloosa, and two times in Hull. In Hull, they performed once to an evening crowd and once during the school day for the students of Western Christian High School.

Calamity Kids featured the adventures of a pair of twins. One of those twins was portrayed by Marv Vande Kieft. For one prank in the play, a cabbage hoisted on a stick served as his head. He recalled, "Every time we did the play, I had to buy a cabbage!"

But what Marv remembers more than buying cabbages is the impact Dad had on his life. A member of Calvary Christian Reformed Church, he was one of the few young people at that church who attended the Pella's community schools rather than its Christian schools. Attendance at Calvary was a difficult experience because he felt like an outsider. But, he said, there were two people who made a difference for him. One was a Calvinist Cadet Corp leader during his grade school years, and the other was Dad—his youth leader and play director during his high school years. Marv said, "As a director, Gary was fantastic. He was patient and caring." Being part of the Dad's theater troupe at Calvary church was a highlight of Marv's youth group experience.

After I had heard about Marv's youth group experience, I shared the story with my friend, Dr. Kara Powell, who is director of the Fuller Youth Institute and author of Growing Young. In her search for the characteristics of churches whose average member age grows younger instead of older, she discovered that these churches have "keychain leaders." A keychain leader decentralizes power and unlocks and empowers young people. When Kara heard the story of Dad and Marv, she immediately said, "Your dad was a keychain leader." Her observation made me even more proud of Dad.

Many people who knew Dad's business side have been stunned to realize he led youth groups and directed theatrical productions. Former Central College president Ken Weller was one of those surprised people. When Ken once remarked on the paradoxes of Dad's character, Dad replied, "I am actually more complicated than you think!"

INCENTIVES AND CONTESTS

When Dad was running the business and working with youth, he loved incentives. He incorporated a contest for the number of tickets cast members sold into each play he directed. In the early years, the top three ticket sellers won an airplane ride to Des Moines, along with dinner in the city.

The system eventually evolved into a two-tier system for winning. All who sold above and beyond a threshold number of tickets won an airplane ride to Des Moines with Dad as the pilot, followed by dinner at the Cloud Room. In the 1950s, the Cloud Room was an upscale restaurant on the upper level of the Des Moines airport terminal. Featuring large windows facing the runways, it was a great place to watch both commercial and private aircraft land and take off. It was a special treat for many youth group members. One menu specialty, a fried shrimp dinner, cost only $1.75. It was one of my favorites! Another option was frog legs, which Dad encouraged many to try.

In the two-tier system, the grand prize for ticket sales was a weekend trip to either Chicago or Grand Rapids, Michigan. Mom accompanied Dad and the two top ticket sellers on those flights.

Selling tickets became very competitive, and parents also helped with sales. Linda De Groot, who had a small part in a play, was one of those top ticket sellers and won a trip to Grand Rapids. Lil Beyer, another member of the youth group at Calvary church, remembers how difficult it was to win one of the prizes. She specifically remembers that since Linda De Groot's father worked for Vermeer, he helped out by selling tickets for her to fellow employees. Linda also remembers Dad as "a good director, always reminding us to project our voices."

Sixty years after the event, when a photo of Dad was posted on Facebook, a former youth group member, Fran Bos, wrote in the comment section:

> *Gary was our youth leader at Calvary CRC in the late 50s. I mostly remember the plays we did…The three people who sold the most tickets got a plane ride to Des Moines and dinner at the airport. My dad, Abe Bos at Pella Corp, really helped me out, and I was always one of the three!*

INCENTIVES FOR WORK

Growing up on the farm, Stan, Bob, and I were all part of Dad's summer work program and incentive plans. Bob remembers helping during hay season, driving the tractor with the small square baler or loading bales on the wagon or onto the elevator to go into the haymow.

I had several jobs in the summer for which I had to keep a time card. At the end of the summer, Dad paid me.

For one job, I picked weeds in the beans in the four-acre field to the south of our home. I also helped during hay baling season. Putting hay up into the barns was not an easy job.[1]

Dad devised a gas-powered system that would pull up a group of square bales through a pulley system into the hay mow. My job was to listen to the commands and pull a lever that put tension on the rope and pulley system to lift up the group of bales into the hay mow. I then had to listen for the command to stop the process and open the fork system to allow the bales to drop into the hay mow. This system was still very labor intensive, with one person forking the bales into a group on the hay wagon beneath the hay mow and another person in the hay mow, placing the bales in an orderly fashion once they were dropped. Stan was often the person in the hay mow—a hot and dirty job. I was quite happy with my pulley responsibility.

Dad paid me seventy-five cents per hour, which was a good wage in the early 1960s. Often at the end of the summer, if I had done a good job he gave me a raise. I must have done a good job every summer!

Dad took this reward system to another level with the multiple young people who were hired in the summer to pick weeds out of the beans in the very large fields of what he called "the north bottom." He had a set hourly wage for each of the young people. A youth with experience was appointed foreman and received a higher wage—a good leadership opportunity. Incentives included perfect attendance and finishing fields ahead of schedule. Hiring young people and encouraging them with a good wage and incentives was a pattern my father used throughout his career.

As Vermeer needed more manufacturing space, the construction of new plants provided another opportunity to hire young people. The company purchased a farm east of Pella for expansion purposes. In 1966, a contractor was hired and construction on the first plant east of town began. Each day, Dad watched the progress, and neither the quality nor the pace of the project pleased him. He decided to manage the project himself, and he terminated the contract.

The company's first plants had a steel and cinder block structure with a brick facing. Rather than hire experienced bricklayers, Dad chose to hire high school and college students. He taught them how to lay brick and then incentivized them to get the work done in a timely fashion. This was great work for students who were saving up for college or a first car.

One of the students who worked on two of the plants was Dale Van Donselaar. In 1966, Dale stopped at the plant manager's office, looking for summer work. Dad was passing by and asked him, "Do you know how to lay block?"

Dale said, "I don't, but I could learn." Dad hired him, and he learned how to lay both block and brick. In 1969, when the second plant was constructed, he became the teacher of block- and brick-laying for the new hires. Dad established a target number of bricks to be laid by each employee. If the goal was exceeded, there was a five-cent bonus per extra brick laid. Dale recalled a record-setting day of laying 690 bricks—definitely in the bonus range.

Dale also remembers a day in 1969 when Dad came by and asked, "Who laid these bricks?"

"I did," Dale responded.

"Wow! Those are nice and straight," Dad said. He enjoyed seeing good work. "Nice and straight" was about as superlative a compliment as anyone ever received from Dad.

PROMOTING PRODUCTS

When Dad invented his first labor-saving device, the mechanical wagon hoist, he sold it to neighbors who needed it. The device mechanically lifted the front of a wagon so the grain could easily flow from the back. The hoists were sold primarily by word of mouth in Marion and the surrounding counties.

Dad decided to take his next invention, the power take-off Pow-R-Drive, to a farm show. He was approached by Connor Flynn, an aspiring young ad agent from Des Moines, about this corn-shelling device. Connor urged Dad to put a full-page ad in the *Wallace's Farmer* magazine to promote his PTO Pow-R-Drive for hammermills and corn shellers.

When Dad asked how much a full-page would cost and found out that it was $1,200, he replied, "That's way too much."

They agreed on a quarter-page ad for $300. The week after the ad first appeared in *Wallace's Farmer*, Dad expected to receive inquiries. After several days of seeing no inquiries in his small postal box, he asked the postmaster if he had seen any mail for him.

The postmaster chuckled, "We have been saving them in the back because there are too many for your postal box!" The postmaster went to the back of the room and returned with a bushel basket filled with thousands of inquiries.

With limited staffing, Dad had no way to even begin to respond to the inquiries, much less do any follow-up work. So he hired someone to help answer inquiries and take orders. At that time, the company employed six people (including Dad) and spent around $1,500 per year on advertising. In an early price list, there were three Pow-R-Drive units offered for sale, ranging in price from $190 to $225 for

Quarter-page ad for the Vermeer Pow-R-Drive

hammermills and $144 to $152 for corn shellers. Over the next decade, 20,000 units were manufactured and sold. These sales were the real boost that gave the company momentum.

Dad also transferred his knowledge of power take-off drives to other inventions, including PTO trenchers (1950) for field tiling, giant PTO boom-type traveling sprinklers for irrigation (1951), and PTO stump cutters (1957).

Probably because of Dad's success with his first quarter-page ad, he developed a theory that the best use of his advertising resources was spending money on promoting new products. Throughout his years at Vermeer, he often questioned what percentage of sales we were spending on advertising. And he always encouraged the company to put that money into showcasing new products. On the other hand, he believed dealerships could and should keep the spotlight on current products.

Over the years, not all management team members have agreed with this policy, but we still take it into consideration when launching new products. Through the decades, those products have included the stump grinder, tree spade, round hay baler, hydrostatic track trenchers, horizontal directional drills, tub and horizontal grinders, surface miners, etc. At one time, each of these products was a new Vermeer entry into the market.

FOCUS

In the book *The Snowball: Warren Buffett and the Business of Life,* business tycoon Warren Buffet tells of a dinner in which the host asked him and Microsoft founder Bill Gates what was the most important attribute of their success. Without conferring, they both gave their host the identical answer: focus.[2]

Dad hadn't read the book, and he never met either Buffet or Gates, but he often said, "You just need to focus on the key issues to get results." He said this whenever we had too much inventory and needed to focus on reducing inventory

The original "ice cream scoop" tree mover

that was tying up cash, or when we had quality issues that needed attention.

Dad also knew that Vermeer's distribution group needed to focus. When the first tree mover was developed in 1964, it looked like a large ice cream scoop. It had only limited success. My uncle, John Vermeer, who was one of the owners of Pella Nursery, tested one of the original tree movers. When I asked him how it worked, he answered honestly, "The chains were always breaking, and it was clumsy."

A new design was needed. In 1967, a four-spade design was successfully worked out. These first units were sold directly from the company to nurseries for transplanting trees.

However, in order to really scale up the sales of these tree spades, focused distribution was needed in our industrial dealer group. John Vander Wert, who was an executive in the sales department at Vermeer, recalls the 1969 sales meeting in Newton, Iowa. Dad announced to the dealer organization that they would be able to represent Vermeer with the new tree spade. However, there was a stipulation: They needed to hire a dedicated tree-spade-only sales person.

To put this in perspective, our total sales volume in 1969 was a little over $8 million. We had twenty-three dealership locations across the United States, most of them carrying only Vermeer products. A staffing requirement such as Dad's is not usually welcomed by dealerships. However, after extended conversations and acquiring a better understanding of the importance of a dedicated specialist for the new tree spade, the majority of the dealers agreed to hire a specialist. The result: Tree spade sales grew rapidly.

Through the 1980s and 1990s, we had multiple discussions about the tree spade line of products. We had developed a product line that moved trees with trunks ranging from four inches to nine inches in diameter. Other lines of equipment, however, grew at a faster rate and volume than trees spades, and we had to evaluate whether it was wise to invest the time needed for design changes, the cost of keeping spare parts on hand, and the cost of maintaining support materials for the tree spade line.

Vermeer produced its last tree spade line—the TS20—in 2012. Our focus went elsewhere.

FOCUS IN DISTRIBUTION

The invention of the large round hay baler in 1971 raised the question of distribution. Members of the management team were not in agreement on how to distribute this new invention. Since we had already started a Vermeer exclusive industrial distribution network, it was certainly one option. However, Dad felt very strongly that our exclusive industrial

The four-spade design that became the foundation for decades of tree spade designs

dealers would not be able to successfully make the leap to the agricultural industry. This network had been selling to the telephone companies and local industrial contractors. Selling to farmers might take a different skill set and focus.

Dad admired the seed corn business system in which farmers sold to other farmers. And that is how the original baler distribution system started. After successful demonstrations of the "one-person hay system," interested farmers were set up to use the Vermeer round baler and to sell it to other local farmers at a ten percent margin. This worked for several years, but eventually evolved into a network of dedicated agricultural dealers who carried parts and performed service. By 2017, we had over four hundred forage dealers who represented Vermeer forage equipment across North America.

FOCUS ON THE CUSTOMER

Dad was intuitive about marketing and definitely had a sense of the importance of focus. But he also had a connection with end users that helped grow the company in the early years.

Dad sometimes got in his plane and flew to see customers who were having issues with our machines. In the first decade, he was known to fly the Beechcraft Bonanza or the Piper Cub to see industrial customers using our trenchers. In the third decade of Vermeer's history, he enjoyed using his helicopter to touch down in a field while a farmer was baling hay.

When he landed, his focus was on listening. Wilbur Van Ryswyk, who worked a variety of Vermeer jobs for our agriculture line, was sometimes assigned to visit customers with service problems. When advising Wilbur about customer interactions, Dad said, "Don't talk a lot. Do a lot of listening.

You will find out that farmers often know what the problem is, and if you listen long enough, they help solve their problem." Dad also advised Wilbur to then immediately go back to the engineering department and work on fixing the issue he had just seen in the field. Dad had a strong sense of urgency to resolve customer issues. Too often we can be quick to defend our product, but for him, listening was key to a win-win resolution.

Several Vermeer team members remember flying with Dad in the helicopter during hay season. He often flew to southern Iowa and northern Missouri, the original demo areas for the launch of the round baler. If he saw our yellow baler in a field, he would land and talk to the farmer. He loved the feedback he got from these end customers on what worked and didn't work.

Landing in a field where a farmer is using a Vermeer baler

Steve Haverly recalled going along on a helicopter ride with Dad in the mid-1980s and landing in a customer field near Prairie City. Steve said, "The customer was in awe that a helicopter had just landed in his field and that Gary Vermeer himself got out of it and talked to him.

Gary loved getting into the field with the hay baler.

"At the end, I apologized to the customer for messing up his windrows of hay because of the outwash of the helicopter. He replied, 'Don't worry about it. This is a story I'll be telling my family and friends!'"

Vermeer Corporation continues to focus on the customer experience. We consciously monitor every aspect of customer interactions with Vermeer Corporation and local Vermeer dealers. When we find instances where we are not meeting our customers' expectations, we focus on countermeasures to improve that aspect of the customer experience. Staying focused and listening to customers were key principals for Dad, and they remain essential to our success in the marketplace.

7 | Practical Leadership

Responsiveness, Simplicity, Boundaries, Goals, and More

Practical business leadership means: understanding economic cycles and how to adjust to them, keeping business simple, being financially sound, setting boundaries around work and non-work time, setting short-term goals, managing by walking around, looking for opportunities, and understanding your key values. Dad modeled leadership in all these areas.

RESPONDING TO ECONOMIC CYCLES

Throughout our history, Dad and the management team have used various steps, or levers, to help the company adjust to economic changes. When Vince Newendorp was manager of forage engineering, downturns happened at the beginning of every decade. He told me, "When things got slow, Gary would say, 'Forty percent of your people have to go back into production until we see profitability.'" This prevented layoffs, but it meant our team members had be flexible. Vince is not sure where Dad's 40 percent figure came from, but it was certainly a step toward reducing GSA&E (General Sales, Administrative, and Engineering) costs.

Cheri Klyn, who has worked in payroll at Vermeer for decades, had a file called the "Gary file." When times were tight, Dad would regularly go to Cheri and ask, "How many people do we have in engineering? How many did we have five years ago? Ten years ago?" Cheri learned to keep that file updated so she always had the information she needed when Dad stopped by. The purchasing group also remembered that when sales were soft, they needed to be prepared to send some of their purchasing team into production until the economy improved and the company could absorb the GSA&E costs.

Dad had no problem advising our dealer group to adjust during downturns in the economy. Doug Wilson, who ran one of the early dealerships in Olathe, Kansas, and continued to work with Vermeer in various capacities throughout his career, recalled a sales meeting at the beginning of the 1970s. At this particular meeting, Dad said, "It looks like it will be a slow year. When times get tough, it is not the time to buy new things. So if your wife is wanting a new refrigerator, but yours works okay, I suggest you use it for another year." Dad was concerned about dealer spending habits. He wanted to be sure dealers had the financial stability to operate through good and bad times. After that admonition, there was speculation whether Matilda ever asked for a new refrigerator, and if she did whether she ever got one!

Dad once described his economic viewpoint this way: "It never gets so good that it won't get worse, and it never gets so bad that it won't get better."

He first said that at a 1980s annual meeting of dealers and owners. Dad started his presentation to the dealer sales group with a story about flying. He had received his pilot's license in 1949, and he regularly flew the corporate planes to see customers and dealers across the country. After flying for thirty years, he also got his instrument rating. He had logged many hours, and he used the flying example to talk about economic ups and downs:

> *I have had it many times that I took off in beautiful, clear weather, but by the time I reached my destination, the weather had changed and I needed to land in instrument weather.*
>
> *There are other times, when I take off in instrument weather, but by the time I get to my destination, the weather has cleared and I can do a visual landing.*

He compared this changeability to business. In economic downturns, it will get worse for a while, but eventually the economy turns a corner and starts to get better. Likewise there have been times when business is fantastic, but that period can be followed by a downturn that requires significant change and adjustments in the organization.

We have used Dad's analogy often through the years; it is a great statement of hope in tough times. In 2001–2003, our company experienced many challenges due to the dot-com crisis. The 1990s had been a big-growth decade for the company. Our sales had tripled, mostly due to the introduction and growth of Horizontal Directional Drills (HDD). We introduced HDD units in 1992, and by the end of the decade nearly 50 percent of our sales were tied to these units. At the end of 2000, the demand for HDD rigs dropped dramatically. Our customers, who were using them to install fiber optics, delayed or cancelled projects.

We had just started to gain momentum with our lean, or continuous improvement, journey. We had eliminated wasted steps in manufacturing processes, enabling us to double our production of HDD units while using the same number of team members. Then the fiber optics economy collapsed, which was followed by 9/11 and the Enron scandal. We used Dad's statement to remind people that we were in "instrument weather." We weren't sure how long the downturn would last, but things would get better.

We knew it was important to always communicate the reality of the situation to our team. We shared with them that inventory levels were high at the dealerships. One of our first tasks was to help our dealers reduce their inventory and financial debt. Through the next couple years, we had to take several additional steps to adjust to the economic conditions. In 2004, we started to see growth again. We were able to restart manufacturing in the HDD plant that we had closed in 2001. We then saw nice growth through 2008.

In 2009, Vermeer and the rest of the country faced another financial crisis, this time on a global scale. Once again, we reminded our team that even after the good growth from 2004–2008 there could always be challenges in the future. After all, "It never gets so good that it won't get worse."

During the 2009 downturn, we were able to make adjustments by reducing inventory on our yard and on our dealers' yards. We focused on a few key engineering projects that could produce more sales in the near future. We reduced hours, but we did not have to reduce our workforce. By the beginning of 2010, we were back to forty-hour work weeks. Several years of outstanding growth followed.

As difficult as the downturn of 2001–2003 was, it was a learning experience that helped us survive the 2009 downturn and start growing again more quickly than many other companies in the industry. By keeping our great team members onboard, we could expand the working hours without needing to hire new team members. Some of our suppliers had difficulty bringing on new people and getting them up to speed soon enough to provide us with the quality parts we needed on a timely basis. Our customers also remarked that they appreciated the fact that Vermeer Corporation and Vermeer dealers continued to service them, communicate with them, and show the importance of the customer relationship through these challenges.

This commitment to our customers resulted in confidence in Vermeer, which helped grow our business in the next years. Our focus on a few key engineering projects resulted in more new products introduced to the industry in the years following 2009. Dad's lessons stay with us today as we encounter changes in the business environment, and we continue to follow the model he set up during the early years of the company.

TAKING IN MORE THAN YOU SPEND

In addition to his instrument weather analogy, Dad had other simple rules that he followed in his life and in his work.

One of them was to stay in business by "taking in more than you spend."

Before we had the Vermeer indoor pavilion, we typically set up a tent with tables and chairs, a speaker's platform, and an amplification system for large meetings. Dad would begin with some welcoming remarks to our guests. Later in his career, Dad often told the story of how he had started Vermeer.

Once I said to him, "Dad, you do such a great job of telling people how you started the company."

His simple reply: "Well…I was there."

Dad's stories of the early days of Vermeer were always a hit with dealers, customers, and reporters. On one occasion, a reporter stood up during a question-and answer session after Dad's opening remarks and asked, "How do you make money?"

Dad responded, "I take in more than I spend."

Laughter rippled through the crowd. When it subsided, Dad asked him, "How do you make money?"

The reporter had no ready retort, and Dad moved on to the next question. That reporter never ventured to ask Dad another question.

Pam Pothoven, who has worked in the finance department and for Vermeer in various capacities for over forty years, was one of the people Dad trusted. If he wanted a quick answer or some numbers tallied, he went directly to Pam.

Pam said that during the uncertain economic time in 2003, Dad came to her desk and said, "I want you to type this out for me. 'What do we do to make money?'"

He then dictated a multi-point answer to the question and asked her to print it and give it to Steve Van Dusseldorp, the chief financial officer. Dad had a good working relationship with Steve, but Steve was out of the office on the day Dad had

Gary giving a presentation at a meeting

Gary speaking at an outdoor meeting. Bob and I are standing on the platform behind him.

these ideas in mind. So he asked Pam to type them out for Steve's return. The document had points about eliminating all unnecessary spending, reducing all wages and salaries, reducing engineering expenses and projects, considering a price increase (only after reducing costs), and keeping lean processes going.

I have used Dad's principle of taking in more than you spend for various speeches and board meetings. It's a simple principle, but sometimes the simple truths are easily forgotten. Often this statement means that if the revenue is not coming in as planned, it is time to cut costs. That is never a pleasant process, but it is one that makes us think about where the real value is in an organization. It also reminds us to think about other ways to increase revenue. In my experience, we have needed to constantly look at ways to increase the top line and as well as ways to reduce costs.

When an executive team is composed of some members who focus internally and others who focus externally, good ideas emerge on how to increase top line and improve the bottom line. We have tried many ideas for top-line generation, including sales-blitz events. Often team members from Vermeer Corporation join forces with a dealership team, and together they canvas an area to find new customers and recommit to current customers. We focus on value-added time with customers, working on making good contacts in a timely fashion.

UNDERSTANDING PEOPLE MANAGEMENT

Dad's philosophy on people was a mix. On one hand, he was an autocratic manager, checking on work and making sure people were held accountable. On the other hand, he really appreciated the people who worked for him.

Dr. Ken Weller, whose doctoral thesis was on enterprise in a free society, told me he enjoyed getting to know Pella's foremost entrepreneurs: Pella Corporation founder Pete Kuyper and Dad.[1] Ken said both men were more concerned about keeping jobs for the people who worked for them during difficult economic times than about making money. Both men knew that to maintain a long-term company, it was necessary to make money. But they both balanced the needs of their employees with the need to reduce costs. Pete is often quoted as saying, "It is the heart of our people that make our windows and doors great."

The flip side of Dad's commitment to people was requiring them to be accountable. Dad was not hesitant to dismiss people from the company. I once sat in a conference room with Dad when he called in an engineer who he didn't think fit our culture. His work ethic was not in alignment with what Dad expected. Dad said to him, "Sometimes the person isn't right for the company, and sometimes the company isn't right for the person."

Dad suggested that the engineer take a week of paid leave to decide if Vermeer was the right place for him or if a different company would be a better fit. Dad didn't list the items that had irritated him about this engineer; he just laid out the option of leaving. The engineer came back a week later having decided he would pursue a different opportunity outside Vermeer. This conversation made a deep impression on me. I saw that Dad was respectful of the person, but he also made it very clear that maybe the fit wasn't right for either of them.

Steve Haverly said he once heard Dad say to a production employee, "You seem unhappy, and I am unhappy. And I can make a difference." In this case, these words were the opening statement in releasing this person from the company. Steve has since used a similar approach when there is an employee who continually complains about his or her job. Steve suggests that the employee has the choice of where to work and that he or she might be happier working elsewhere.

Tony Vis, a former pastor at Meredith Drive Reformed Church in Des Moines, once emphasized a similar point in a sermon. He said, "If you are unhappy in your work, you really have two options: either change your attitude or change your work." The option that too many people take is to do neither. Instead, they stay in their job and complain.

Bill Vander Molen, one of Vermeer's first salespeople, helped start a lot of Vermeer industrial dealerships. When I began working in the company in 1982, he was still helping dealerships establish best practices and occasionally stopped at my office. He often told me the same message—one that he also told his dealer mentees: "There are two things that are crucially important if you want to be successful: attitude and communication." I have learned that Bill was right. If people have a positive attitude, can find good in most situations, and are able to effectively communicate, they have a very good chance of not only being successful in their work, but enjoying it.

SHORT-TERM GOALS

Dad was rarely involved in setting goals; in fact, he didn't like long-term goals. I think he had lived through so many ups and downs in the economy—including the Great Depression—that he believed it was more important to focus on the present and on achieving short-term goals. He certainly had a lot of short-term targets connected with a season of selling equipment or a project he wanted to get done. And he liked leading a team or his family in accomplishing short-term goals—such as hiking the Grand Canyon.

Dad and Mom had hiked down the Grand Canyon multiple times with friends and family. They enjoyed hiking down one of the trails, staying at Phantom Ranch along the Colorado River, and then hiking up the other trail on the way out. In 1989, during spring break, we made a family hike down the canyon. Dad was seventy, and David Vermeer, the youngest in the family, was seven. After a hearty breakfast, we started our adventure hiking down Bright Angel Trail. After hiking over ten miles down that trail, we second-generation Vermeer family members were all very tired when we got to Phantom Ranch. The third generation had lots of energy, and Mom and Dad seemed very comfortable. Since they had done this trek before, they had been disciplined in training for the hike. Dad had found the steepest and longest hill around Pella, which is several miles west of town on a gravel road. They trekked up and down that hill multiple times per week, preparing their bodies for the hike.

After a good rest in dormitory-type lodging and a large breakfast, we started the ascent. On the way out of the Canyon, we took the 7.5-mile South Kaibab Trail. The Kaibab Trail was steeper, but shorter. On both trails, Dad led the troupe. The rest of us just fell into line in random order. Dad paced us. He would count one hundred steps; then we would all rest, proceed another hundred steps, and then rest again. This was a very effective way to bring the entire group out of the canyon safely and in good shape. Dad was definitely the leader in achieving our short-term goals of reaching Phantom Ranch and climbing out to the South Rim.

In 2002, Dale and I, along with Jason and Mindi, thought it would be great to do that same trek with our nuclear family. At Thanksgiving, Jason and Carrie had been married a little over two years, and Frank and Mindi had just celebrated their one-year anniversary. We decided to take the trails in reverse order, walking down the 7.5-mile South Kaibab to Phantom Ranch and then taking the 10-mile Bright Angel Trail up. That was a definite mistake. Even though South Kaibab is steeper, the extra 2.5 miles of Bright Angel took a real toll on our hiking endurance.

Another challenge greeted us on our trip out of the canyon: It started snowing about three miles from the top. Even though overall the trail wasn't as steep, it was still plenty steep in the last thousand feet. Between the snow, the steepness of the trail, and the poor shape of the steps on the trail, Dale and I began to wonder if we would make it to the top by evening. At one point, Dale suggested—half seriously—that if he broke a leg, maybe a helicopter would come and take him off the trail. We decided to send Frank, Carrie, and Mindi on ahead. The loads of our backpacks were divided among our children and their spouses. Jason stayed with us, and we used Dad's pacing method. However, we only took fifty steps before resting! Watching Dad's leadership while hiking the Canyon

Gary pacing the family on the trek from Phantom Ranch to the South Rim

The family taking a well-deserved break from hiking

showed us the importance of pacing ourselves—or a group—through a difficult challenge.

When I called Mom and told her about our difficult trek out of the canyon, she said, of course, that we had taken the wrong route. She and Dad had found out that it was much better to take the steeper Kaibab out of the Canyon! In our planning, we should have consulted with Mom, a veteran of hiking the Canyon.

Gary leading the way on South Kaibab Trail

KEEP IT SIMPLE

When a lot of paper was handed out at a meeting, Dad would always ask, "How many trees are we killing today?" It wasn't that he believed we should be paperless; the electronic devises were not part of his world. But he liked simplicity, so he thought one piece of paper should be enough to make a point.

He asked the same question of attorneys. He often commented that wills and contracts were too many pages. "Why can't they put it all on one page?" he would ask.

Nelson Nikkel, known by most people as Nick, was in charge of Vermeer procurement for many years. In the mid-1980s, when we were not making any money with our rubber tire product line, Dad suggested we should just quit making rubber tire trenchers. We held a meeting with many of the dealer principals. In discussions, they loudly disagreed with Dad's suggestion. They maintained that the rubber tire trenchers were a basic unit necessary to retain their customer base.

Dad decided we should separate out the rubber tire products and put them into a separate division that could experiment with different methods for lowering overhead cost. A few people were asked if they would like to apply for the top management of the Rubber Tire (RT) division. Nick applied. The business plan he submitted was simple—just one paragraph. Another applicant presented a formal business plan of multiple pages.

Nick got the job. Dad was looking for a simple, to-the-point, and focused perspective.

The decision to separate out that product line worked. We are still in the utility trencher business, and we now understand the importance of maintaining a group of core machines that are critical to the viability of our dealer groups. The RT division also experimented with several of Dad's other ideas. He thought it might be better to just focus on one R&D project at a time and get that one project done faster. For the first several years, the small engineering group focused on just one new machine per year. Dad loved experimenting with ideas, and the RT Division actually spun off three other divisions: OEM (Original Equipment Manufacturer), SP (Specialty Products), and AT^2 (Ag, Track, and Tree).

The simplicity principle also applied to machine design. Vince Newendorp worked for many years with Dad. When designing a new machine, Dad made it clear that it would be best if the parts on a machine could be purchased at the lumber or hardware store, since that would be the simplest solution for our customers. Dad stated, "I want customers to find the parts locally."

Many of our designs for directional drills in China use the same principle. If our customers can find spare parts easily in their local areas in China—and we design a simple machine—we have a better chance to gain more of the market share. In China, we offer both the American-designed products and a C series, which is designed with locally available Chinese parts.

Vince recalled that the industrial engineering group once bought a couple of AutoCADs (software for machine design) for their design work. The industrial and forage engineering groups were located in different plants because our goal was to always keep engineers close to the plants that produced the products they designed.

Later, Vince brought one of the AutoCAD systems over to the forage design group. When Dad, who was skeptical of computers, saw the AutoCAD in the forage engineering group, he asked for a contest. He asked Vince to put his best CAD operator on the system to compete with him in a pencil-versus-computer challenge. He requested a drawing of a ¼-inch by 2-inch bar stock, 12 inches long, and with a ½-inch diameter hole, 1 inch from each end.

Dad sat with his pad of paper, the best AutoCAD operator sat at the keyboard, and the contest began. Of

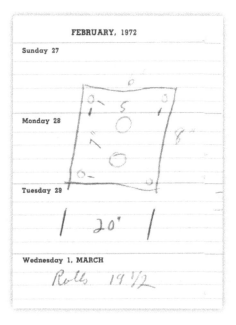

One of Gary's drawings

course, Dad won. His point was: If something simple needs to be made, use paper.

Eventually, Vince was able to convince Dad that for many complex designs, computer-aided design (CAD) was a better alternative.

But Dad had made his point: simpler is usually better!

DEBT

Dad often said a farmer should buy a farm only if he had fifty percent of the purchase price in cash. Then it would be reasonable to expect that in the near future, the farm could produce enough income to pay back the rest of the loan. Jacob, his father, had been a bank shareholder and director following the Great Depression, and he had seen foreclosures on many farms. Dad likely learned from his father that the farmers who were highly leveraged were the ones who lost their farms during that time. Seeing farmers lose their farms, and often their dignity as well, had made an impression on Dad. He hated debt.

Despite that aversion, in 1973 the company needed a loan in order to increase production from 300 to 3,300 balers in one year. Even with $500 deposit per baler order (required in the early days of baler manufacture), he would need additional financing for payroll and for purchases of material.

John Vander Wert suggested they might need to borrow $1 million from Iowa Des Moines National Bank. Dad and John traveled to Des Moines and met with the bank president. He took out a notepad and wrote "Loan to Vermeer $1 Million." The president asked Dad to cosign the note, and the paperwork was complete. The loan started in September, and Vermeer had paid it off by the following March. In those five months, Dad stopped at John's office regularly and asked, "How much is paid off?"

Dad also accepted the need for short-term debt, which is sometimes essential for cash flow. The spring season can often be a tight-cash period. We are producing machines, but haven't sold enough of them for adequate cash flow. In several years, we have used short-term debt to help with cash needs. But over the course of our seventy years in business, long-term debt has been minimal.

BOUNDARIES

Striking a healthy work-life balance isn't easy, and maintaining distinct boundaries between your work and your personal life is the topic of many business lectures, articles, and discussions. For most people in business, the lines often get blurred. With 24/7 digital communication, it is not easy to turn off work when you move into your personal and family time.

Dad seemed to be able to clearly differentiate between work and non-work time. Daryl Van Zee, a long-term team member who worked with Dad in agricultural engineering, told me about a fishing trip to Canada with Dad. Daryl was also a pilot, so Dad asked him to be his copilot in the front right seat. After takeoff, Dad said, "We have a few things we need to talk about on your work project. We will talk about this until we hit the Iowa-Minnesota state line, and then we won't talk more business." And that is exactly what happened. They discussed the project until the airplane flew over the state line. After that, there was no more talk about business.

As this example shows, Dad definitely knew how to set boundaries. At work, he was focused and driven by results, but away from work he was social, connected, and willing to let events evolve.

Rich Shelton, a long-term Vermeer team member, remembers going to the camp north of town with a group of office employees for water skiing, volleyball, and hamburgers grilled by Dad. He said when someone wanted to discuss a work issue with Dad, his reply was, "We don't need to talk about work now."

Dad also loved the old tradition of *shivaree*—surprising a newlywed couple with an early-morning breakfast. He organized *shivaree* events for friends and for a few engineering team members at Vermeer. One of the newlywed engineering couples at Vermeer was Vince and Monica Newendorp. Dad planned the schedule. They left the plant at 5:30 a.m. with everything needed to fix breakfast: pans, eggs, bacon, juice, and coffee. They arrived at the Newendorp home at 5:45. After they rang the doorbell multiple times, Vince opened the door. Dad pushed past him and announced, "Breakfast will be ready in fifteen minutes. Get Monica up so she can join us."

Once inside, everyone was assigned a task and went to work. Although Monica admittedly was not an early-morning person, she joined the special breakfast. Both newlyweds enjoyed the surprise, the food—and seeing Dad in total charge of the kitchen.

At 6:30, Dad announced clean-up time so they would not be late for work. At 6:45, the traveling breakfast troupe of nearly a dozen engineering personnel left the house and headed back to Vermeer to start their day at 7:00. Steve Haverly, part of the breakfast group, remembers how much Dad smiled and joked around with everyone during the *shivaree*. But once he was at work, he switched immediately to work mode.

MANAGEMENT BY WALKING AROUND

Anecdotes about Dad walking though the Vermeer plants abound. He often walked to the engineering area to check on a project or to pick up something that had been made for one of his farm projects. As he walked, if he noticed something he considered questionable, he stopped to inquire.

Whenever he saw two people talking he stopped to listen, but if three people were talking, he doubted they were focused on their work. He stopped, asked their names, the name of their supervisor—and then suggested they get back to work. I do not know whether he always followed up with the supervisor, but I am sure he made mental notes about those individuals.

There are several classic stories of snowballs flying through the plants during the winter. When fixtures were brought in from the outside with snow on them, it was very tempting to make a snowball. Once, Dad exited his office as one of the team members was throwing a snowball and Dad was nearly hit by it. He looked at the culprit and asked, "What is your name? Who is your boss?"

Then he added, "You need to get back to work."

One observer of the near-miss said, "Gary wasn't really upset. He was just matter-of-fact."

Another often-repeated story is that an in-plant snowball once hit Dad in the face. In that case, the thrower left the company grounds with a three-day pass.

Rich Shelton recalled seeing Dad in the plants often. He said, "Gary didn't walk in to spy. He came because he had something to do, but he observed and noticed things."

When I was about nine or so, I sometimes went along to the plant on the west side of Pella after evening meetings. We would often talk to the security person, and Dad would check on a project. My cousin Nancy, eldest daughter of Harry Vermeer, also remembers walking the plants with her dad. Harry was Dad's youngest brother who joined the company in the early 1950s as part-owner.

In the early days of the company, it was easier to walk into a manufacturing plant without steel-toed shoes, hearing protection, or safety glasses. In addition, there were no restrictions on children's presence in the plants. Today, we live and work by different rules.

Several team members recall Dad walking in the plants with his hands behind his back. To some, that meant all was well. Others thought his posture showed he was observing and thinking. Through years of observing Dad, Steve Haverly reached a conclusion about the difference between Dad's walking with his hands behind his back or at his side. Steve decided that when Dad entered the engineering department with his hands at his side, he was focused and arriving to get something done. When his hands were behind his back, Steve believed Dad was in "normal walking mode."

Walking through the plants is inherent to managing a manu-facturing firm—or perhaps any company. "Management by wandering around" is a term coined by Tom Peters, commonly referred to as MBWA. MBWA is a style of business in which managers wander through workplaces at random to check on employees, equipment, or the status of ongoing work.[2] Before the term was officially coined, Dad and Harry both walked through the plants to check on projects, to wish employees a happy birthday, or simply to get a pulse of the team.

Today, we continue to understand the importance of walking through our plants. Personally, I have found that walking the plants and chatting with managers and people on the line is a great way to connect with our team. I once sat next to Art Byrne, one of the early lean process gurus, at a luncheon. We were just beginning our lean manufacturing journey. He told me:

> *If Vermeer is going to get engaged in the lean journey, every month you personally need to work on one **kaizen** event [a week-long team event focused on a specific improvement]. You will understand the strengths and weaknesses of your people, your products, and your processes better by participating in events than by anything else that you do.*

I didn't reach his target, but I participated in twelve events in the first two years of our lean journey. I did find that getting to know more of our team members by working with them at events added to my ability to connect with a variety of people as I walked the plants. Participating in *kaizen* events is an important part of learning and getting input on how work is going and the temperature of the workforce. They are also an opportunity to assure the team members that they are valued.

LOOKING FOR OPPORTUNITIES

Dad loved to build manufacturing plants. If we had extra cash, he thought it was wise to build the next plant so we could be ready for the next opportunity to build new equipment. In the years when Dad was involved with production, there was never a big downturn. In 1985, we built what is now Plant 5 to be ready for the next equipment opportunity. However, there wasn't much growth in the rest of that decade, and the space was not needed for production. For a while, we stored corn in Plant 5. That was not ideal because cleaning out the corn fibers was a difficult task.

So in the early 1990s, we looked for better opportunities for using that space. We pursued manufacturing items for other companies. I flew with Dad to John Deere in Dubuque to discuss the possibility of Vermeer manufacturing the JD scraper. We were awarded that contract and other OEM (Original Equipment Manufacturer) work. We even carved out a special group to focus on OEM products, OEM manufacturing, and all related back-office tasks. Taking the initiative to find additional products for OEM work, we eventually manufactured OEM products for Fiat, John Deere, and Caterpillar.

Over the years, I heard Dad say the word "opportunity" much more often than the word "problem." That is a mark of a leader. Dad saw opportunities where others only saw problems.

COMPANY PRINCIPLES

In the twenty-fifth anniversary Vermeer Corporation brochure, which was published in 1973, Dad laid out his key beliefs about the company focus:

Often the success of a business is attributed to hard work, sincerity, honesty, and diligent effort. Certainly these characteristics have marked our business. However, at Vermeer there are essentially three basic principles that are equally important. First, there must be well-engineered, thoroughly tested, and marketable products. Secondly, a strong, loyal, and competent organization must be developed to sell and service the products, because at Vermeer, we believe service at all levels is of utmost importance. After the first two principles have been realized, then there must be good manufacturing facilities and quality-conscious people available to build the products.

When I started at the company in 1982, I remember an employee asking, "We always knew what your Dad believed was important in the company, but what about you kids?" At that point, Stan, Bob, and I were all part of the business, and we were often called "the kids." Stan had put some goals and boundaries together, and I realized that it was important for our team to have a simple way to remember our foundational values. I took pieces of the writing Stan had started and used four Ps to make them easy to remember. I started talking

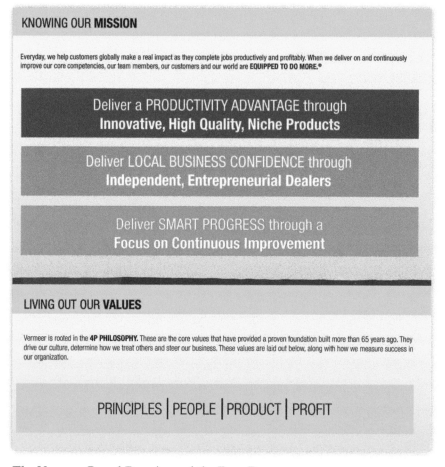

KNOWING OUR MISSION

Everyday, we help customers globally make a real impact as they complete jobs productively and profitably. When we deliver on and continuously improve our core competencies, our team members, our customers and our world are **EQUIPPED TO DO MORE.®**

Deliver a PRODUCTIVITY ADVANTAGE through
Innovative, High Quality, Niche Products

Deliver LOCAL BUSINESS CONFIDENCE through
Independent, Entrepreneurial Dealers

Deliver SMART PROGRESS through a
Focus on Continuous Improvement

LIVING OUT OUR VALUES

Vermeer is rooted in the **4P PHILOSOPHY.** These are the core values that have provided a proven foundation built more than 65 years ago. They drive our culture, determine how we treat others and steer our business. These values are laid out below, along with how we measure success in our organization.

PRINCIPLES | PEOPLE | PRODUCT | PROFIT

The Vermeer Brand Promise and the Four Ps

about the four Ps to our team members, retail customers, and dealers…and it seemed to stick!

We are focused on managing the business according to biblically based **principles**. We believe our **people** must be treated with dignity and respect. We must design, produce, and support **products** that are innovative, safe, and made with quality. And we must reinvest **profits** into the business to be a long-term business. These four Ps are based on Dad's philosophies and have been the foundation of our values for the last thirty years. However, they truly reflect the company's values for the last seventy years.

The four Ps are just one example of Dad's early philosophy being honored and carried forward to future generations, and our shareholders continually remind the management team that these principles form a standard they want us always to value and honor.

8 | Lean Processes
Using Lean Principles Before Learning the Term

The lean journey at Vermeer officially started in 1998. With our focus on trenchless technology, we had seen a lot of growth in the 1990s. The company sales more than tripled that decade after we entered the trenchless market and grew the business. To accommodate the growth in sales, we increased our number of team members and our inventory. We also added new plants and capital equipment.

We had previously been doing a significant amount of work for other manufacturers like Fiat, Caterpillar, and John Deere. In some cases, we manufactured a whole product. In others, we produced weldments. But as our Vermeer sales grew due to Horizontal Directional Drilling, we realized it was a better to use our space and equipment for our own Vermeer products. So through the 1990s, we began to disengage from our OEM contracts and focus on Vermeer-designed equipment.

Dad had transitioned to the role of Chair Emeritus in 1989. My brother, Bob, had been named CEO, and I had been named president and COO.

In spite of the good growth in sales, we had not seen improvement in the gross margin or net operating margin. We brought in a consulting company who led us through a strategic planning process that identified a big opportunity for improvement: reducing the cost of manufacturing.

At this time, we also had two independent board members. One was from HNI, a subsidiary of HON Industries, which is headquartered in Muscatine, Iowa. He had been involved in their adoption of lean process management, a business strategy long-term continuous improvement and gradual changes that improve manufacturing efficiency and quality. At board meetings, he regularly told us that we could not expect any improvement in the bottom line if we continued to build new plants and add capital equipment and team members to the payroll. With his encouragement, during the 1996 strategic planning meeting we started to explore what it would mean for us to embark on a lean process journey.

At this point, Dad still attended all board meetings, and he was very interested in new products. In particular, he was extremely interested in the concept of Horizontal Directional Drilling, but he was no longer involved in the engineering process or strategy meetings. However, when we decided we needed to approach manufacturing from a lean perspective, he heard our thoughts and direction at board meetings.

In retrospect, Dad had exhibited many of the lean principles in both his personal and work life. He often asked questions and was open to the need to change. However, he wasn't familiar with the prescribed methodology that would really start us on the journey.

When we started the Vermeer lean journey, Dad and I made a visit to our colleagues at Pella Corporation to learn about their lean processes. Pella Corporation had been on their lean journey for several years. We talked to Operations Vice President Mel Haught, who later became CEO. Mel hosted us on a tour of one of their plants, explaining what they had done to improve their processes. The most impactful thing Mel did was draw a timeline on a marker board. The timeline showed that in manufacturing, we often add value to a product for a few minutes; then it sits or it gets moved. The white space, or time when no value is added, is much greater than the value-added time. By working to eliminate the white spaces, we could improve our cost of manufacturing. Dad liked the ideas; however, he left it to his children to oversee the next steps. But as I worked on the lean journey, I realized that many of Dad's personal and business principles aligned well with the lean principles I was learning about.

EVERYTHING IN ITS PLACE FOR FISHING TRIPS

One of the foundations of lean processes is workplace organization. Dad practiced that in his daily life. He talked about how to tell which farmers were good farmers—just by looking at their farms. If they took good care of their farm equipment and stored it in an orderly manner, they were probably successful farmers. Having everything in its place was a good thing!

Everything-in-its-place was a way of life for Dad—on his farm, in the plants, and even on Canadian vacations. For forty years, my parents flew to Canada in the summer, transferring from a land plane to a seaplane on the Rainy River at Baudette, Minnesota, and continuing on to the camp near Perrault Falls, Canada. Once we were settled at the camp, which was about 150 miles north of the Canadian border, there was a meticulous system for fishing.

Since Mom and Dad often took family and friends on three- or four-day fishing excursions, there was a great need for workplace organization. In a building next to the camp's dock was a tack room where they could keep gear

The tack room at the camp

for fishing—fishing rods, dip net, minnow bucket, hip boots, rain gear, tackle box, etc. Each item had its place in the tack room. Every time they came back from a fishing expedition, they unloaded items from the seaplane and put them in exactly the correct spot in the tack room.

Even more remarkable was Dad's organizational system in the floats of the seaplane. When they used an inflatable boat to try out new lakes, they needed to pack the following into the small seaplane: the boat, a compressor for inflating it, boxes for boat seats, and boat seat cushions. And that doesn't even cover the long list of fishing gear. In his early trips to Canada, Dad realized the floats of the seaplane had a lot of empty space he could use for carrying items out to the remote lakes. So, before it became standard in seaplanes, he created openings in each float and then designed a float cover that would keep the float from filling with water. The

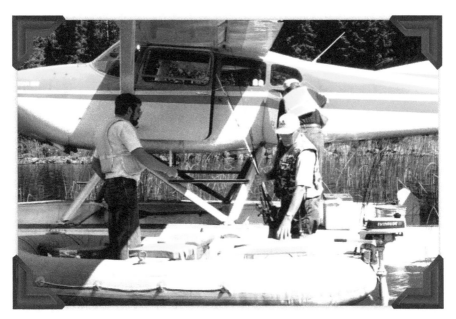

Preparing the inflatable boat

dimensions of the opening were crucial because of the many items that had to be carefully inserted and removed. Dad designed the boxes to nest inside each other and to go nicely through the opening of the float.

He created a prescribed way to load the rods into the middle and back of the plane to prevent tangles. The entire process of loading the floats and the plane interior was a great example of standard work. (In lean methodology, standard work is simply a list of steps you should follow in order each time you are doing a process.) The motor for the boat always went into the floats first, then the boxes (if they were using the inflatable boat). The minnow bucket with live minnows went in last. There were some variations for loading the plane because they didn't need the boat, the compressors, the boxes, or the cushions when they weren't using the inflatable boat.

Often, we went to Sharp Lake—one of our favorites that had a dock built by Dad and others…and that often had to be rebuilt after the winter ice had damaged it. At Sharp, we didn't need hip boots. But at many of the other lakes, such as Lake Matilda, we anchored the plane in a cove by tying it with ropes to trees on land. Then at least one person had to put on hip boots to wade through the shallow water to secure the plane to a sturdy tree with a rope.

A highlight for all fishing groups was shore lunch. That meant we needed to take a skillet, flour mixture for breading the fish, pork and beans, and fruit or cookies along for the lunch. Mom was in charge of taking either the sandwiches for lunch aboard the boat or the extra things we needed for shore lunch. Sharp Lake was the best place for shore lunch since my parents had placed a storage bin on the land near the

Lake Matilda

On one fishing trip with Dad and another guest, Dale and Bob fished a new-to-them lake that was several miles long and a mile wide. It had no name on Dad's aerial maps.

In Iowa, this would have been a very big lake and certainly would have had a name. But in Canada, it is considered small, so it didn't have one. Bob and Dale decided to name it "Lake Matilda" after their mom and mother-in-law.

Later, the camp owner asked the Canadian authorities if that particular lake could officially receive this name. Today, it is called Lake Matilda on the aerial maps.

Lake Matilda, which features two rocky islands, was a frequented stop on our fishing trips. There were great fishing spots, but we also lost a lot of tackle snagging on the rocks between those two islands.

dock. The bin held the camp stove for cooking fish. Dad had constructed two tables between trees. One table was the fish-cleaning area, and the other one held the camp stove for cooking.

Although Mom and Dad had standard processes for all these activities, there were a few occasions when we forgot something. Forgetting the skillet for shore lunch or forgetting the dip net were two of the most disastrous

The all-important dip net used to catch bigger fish

Gary preparing shore lunch on Sharp Lake

omissions—these meant we had lunch without fish or missed landing a big northern pike.

Another standard process for fishing was a *doekje* (pronounced "DUE-key" in Pella, Iowa, and "DUKE-yah" in the Netherlands). A *doekje* is a small rag that we used to hold on to slimy northern pikes or walleyes. The *doekje* was important for holding the fish while getting the hook out of its mouth. The person at the center of the boat was responsible for taking fish from hooks and either releasing them back into the lake or putting them on the stringer. Mom was usually that person. She also handed out minnows from the minnow bucket so each of us could get back to fishing. Many of us learned her job over the years and sometimes sat in that middle seat.

Just as with shore lunch omissions, sometimes the crucial *doekje* didn't make the trip. On one trip, my son, Jason, went fishing alone with his grandparents—and they left the *doekje* behind. Grandma's turned to her husband and grandson and admonished, "Surely, you didn't leave the *doekje* on the dock!" For fishing trips, we didn't have a written checklist for our standard processes, but we all had mental checklists—and sometimes the mental model failed us.

Most of the time, though, following a checklist enabled my parents' fishing groups to have all the correct equipment for a fishing expedition. In lean processes, team members need to have all the right pieces and tools—and follow the most effective steps—in order to do their jobs accurately and in a timely manner.

ORGANIZATION AT THE DUCK BLIND

In the late 1950s, Dad bought a camp property with a half-mile-long pond a few miles north of Pella from John Vanden

Gary and Stan cleaning fish

The family enjoying shore lunch

Noord. It had been built by the owners of Maytag, who had used it as a hunting camp. Dad bought it for duck hunting, but it soon became a great place for gatherings with lots of summer water skiing, hamburger fries, and volleyball games.

Hunting ducks requires a duck blind. Many blinds are simple barriers which conceal hunters from the ducks. Dad created a wonderful blind for his camp. It had a place for four or five hunters to sit and watch for the ducks and geese. Behind this space was a ten-foot-square underground kitchen. It housed a camp stove, water pump, small table, and chairs to enjoy breakfast before or after hunting.

Much like the tack room in Canada, everything had its assigned place in the kitchen of the duck blind. Although Dad was not a cook at home, in the duck blind he always fried the bacon, eggs, and pancakes. And he was very methodical about putting his cooking utensils back in their assigned locations.

Matilda and Gary in the duck blind kitchen

SELF-DISCIPLINE

When I was landing the Bonanza on the airstrip between the plants on the Vermeer campus, Dad often asked me, "Why can't you land on the center line?" Located between Plants 1 and 2, the strip was 2,000 feet long and 24 feet wide, which is very narrow for a landing strip. I thought landing on the cement strip without going onto the adjoining grass was a good landing, but it didn't meet Dad's standards. Although he never verbalized the reason for his landing-on-the-center-line standard, I think he did not want me to risk a grass landing and possibly damage the plane. His philosophy was good discipline—a standard for the work of piloting.

A distant Vermeer cousin, Glenda VerMeer Vander Leest, told me when her father taught her to plow a field, he was adamant about making precise turns at the end of the field. We concluded our Dutch-perfectionist heritage must have influenced our Dads' standards for landing planes and plowing!

To Dad, timeliness was another part of being disciplined. Steve Haverly, who started with Vermeer in 1981 as one of our first engineers with a college degree, often worked with Dad. One product that Dad and the Vermeer team worked on tirelessly—without ever getting it to production—was a tractor-mounted corn picker. Dad really wanted to provide a less expensive machine for harvesting corn than the combine, which was used only a few weeks per year.

Steve remembered it this way:

During the corn-picker days, we were working on a corn sheller attachment. In a design review, we identified changes that needed to be made. The changes required a total rebuild of the attachment. Gary set the completion date six weeks out.

We planned to go to the bottom [a farm north of Pella that was all river bottom ground] to try the new attachment out at noon on a specific day.

I redesigned and built the new attachment, incorporating all the desired changes. On the specified day, I left the factory at noon. By 3:00 p.m., we were running corn through the new sheller. We shut the unit down at 5:00 p.m.

It worked better than we thought it would, and I thought I would be getting an "attaboy" from Gary. Instead, when Gary came up to me, all he said was, "Too bad you didn't meet the deadline."

In that moment, I understood what meeting a deadline was supposed to be, and I have worked with that intention ever since. It is why I get a bit animated when others miss their deadlines—especially when I've been very specific about it. Every once in a while, I will tell that story in an effort to get people to understand how critical deadlines are. Gary recognized that time is a non-renewable resource and deadlines have meaning.

Missing a six-week deadline by just three hours was a very high standard. Dad could be tough!

Discipline is a bedrock in lean processes, and it is not easy. For workplace organization, lean uses the five Ss: sort, set in order, shine, standardize, and sustain. A plant walkthrough immediately reveals whether the discipline of workplace organization is practiced. If kit carts and paint carts are in designated, marked spots, there is a culture of discipline. One of our consultants constantly reminded us, "Never walk over paper." In other words, if there is a piece of paper in a walk aisle, it is important to pick it up and throw it away or put it in an appropriate place. Walking over paper or trash shows others in the area a lack of concern about workplace organization. Just as the center line is an important discipline in flying, or meeting a deadline is an important accomplishment, the disciplines of sustaining an organized workplace and following standard work procedures are crucial in the lean journey.

BASIC METRICS

In lean, we have learned the importance of using basic metrics to mark progress or point to areas that need extra focus. Dad had a simple formula that he used to measure the health of the business: his 20/10/10 metric. For him, ideal capital in the business was twenty percent in inventory, ten percent in fixed assets, and ten percent in receivables. Too much inventory and/or receivables would tie up too much cash. The forty percent investment meant a stable company that could weather tough times and focus on long-term success.

How did Dad develop his metric theories? Certainly he learned through his own experience and by watching trends. In addition, John Vander Wert said he and Dad met with Pella Corporation founder Pete Kuyper in his office several times and in his home at least twice. John recalled, "Gary asked him business questions, especially about inventory turns and business ratios." John and I concluded that Pete's input probably also shaped Dad's standards.

John also remembers that Pete, who was also very direct but more of a marketer than Dad, talked about predicting downturns. Pete was able to project out one to three years, but Gary and John agreed that in Vermeer's industry, it was not possible to predict more than six months out.

Pella Windows and Pete Kuyper

Pella Corporation was founded in 1925—two decades before Vermeer Corporation—when Pete Kuyper and his wife, Lucille, bought Rolscreen Company for $5,000. Rolscreen was based in Des Moines and sold window screens that could be rolled out of sight when not in use.

In 1926, the company moved to Pella, where the Kuypers had a lumber business. In the years since, Pella Corporation has become one of the largest window manufacturers in the United States.

Pella Corporation and Vermeer Corporation are two of Pella's leading employers.[1]

Dad was adamant that dealerships should not be highly leveraged. He feared that during tough economic times, dealerships might not survive if too leveraged. That proved to be true in the dot-com downturn of 2001–2003. Through that period, we had several dealerships which did not have enough capital in the business to survive the severe downturn. Those dealerships were either incorporated into a neighboring dealer or taken over by Vermeer Corporation. As a result, we worked with dealers to get them all to a 25–30 percent capitalization rate. That has proven to be a healthy requirement.

Today, one of our business goals is related to ROCE (Return on Capital Employed). ROCE is calculated as earnings before interest and tax/capital employed. Our ideal is 25 percent ROCE, which aligns with Dad's original 20/10/10 formula.

NEVER PASS A BAD PART

Dad didn't use a specific system for quality management, but he did believe that we needed to deliver reliable, quality equipment to customers. He also believed each person in the manufacturing process needed to be making their own quality checks. He compared it to the highway system. It would be impossible for every driver to be watched by the highway patrol. Likewise, if every piece had to be inspected by a separate person, you would need one quality inspector for every manufacturing person!

Dad's thinking was very much in line with the lean mantra "Never pass a bad part." As an integral part of our lean journey today, we write quality checks into our standard work processes and equip operators with the tools and training to do their job correctly.

Our first self-propelled Tulip Time float

Little things can make a big difference in quality. When we designed and built the first self-propelled Tulip Time float, Dad was quite impressed that we were able to complete the float on time and that it made it through the entire parade route without breaking down.

The first self-propelled float had a Care Bear theme. The designer was Rich Shelton, who enjoyed creating those early self-propelled floats. Rich said Dad came to inspect the float before the evening parade on the first day of the festival. Rich watched Dad look under the float from the side and then look under the float from the back.

Rich thought, *I wonder what he is looking for.* Later he learned Dad had talked with the track engineering team that afternoon and asked, "How is it that our float doesn't have hydraulic leaks, but our track machines always seem to have leaks?"

When Rich heard that story, he realized exactly what Dad was doing looking for under the float—leaks!

Dad was cautious about overusing electronics. He enjoyed electronics in his tractor and airplane, but he always maintained that electronics on our trenchers had to be reliable. If electronics couldn't be reliable, it was better to keep the trenchers simple.

Our customers' perception of quality is proportional to the reliability of their equipment. As a result, we are very conscious of the importance of each seemingly small adjustment, torque, fastener, and electronic feature.

TRYSTORMING

Dad believed in trying new ideas for products. He often said, "If at least 50 percent of your attempts haven't failed, you haven't tried enough." He relished telling stories about all the product ideas they tried at Vermeer that had failed. He would tell about the gravedigger that dug its own grave, the hay conditioner that was before its time, the double baler that didn't catch on, and the tractor-mounted corn picker that never found its niche.

In lean processes, we now use something similar called "trystorming." When we are working on new designs, we get into small groups during a *kaizen* event and come up with five to seven ideas on how to design part of a machine more effectively and with more innovation. We also try to do a rapid simulation of the design so we can evaluate it visually. We trystorm various methods. Often, we end up combining the methodology of three or four of the designs to arrive at the best solution.

Steve Haverly remembers making changes on the corn harvester stalk ejectors. After a lot of debate, Dad wanted to implement his personal choice for a change, even though there were a number of concerns about that design. So they field tested his design and another one simultaneously, one on each of the two corn harvester elevators. When they stopped the picker and climbed up to inspect the results, Dad's design hadn't worked at all; it had caused the elevator to plug. The other side, although it had some disadvantages, had not plugged.

"He compared the two sides, looked at the side that was his idea, turned to look at us, and said, 'Well, that didn't work. Let's go back to the shop and try another idea,'" Steve recalled. "You never got into trouble if something didn't work, unless Gary had told you not to do something or it had already been proven not to work."

Dad was fine with a little competition in design. In fact, he liked it. Under him, engineers competed to see what

Arnie Mathes (pictured) was integral to the development of the hay baler.

worked in the field. Overall, his process was similar to the trystorming of designs that happens in the lean process.

Dad's idea of trying things and failing was to fabricate a "mule" to see if the product design was workable. Mules were the basis for many Vermeer innovations. Probably the most notable product that exhibited the mule process was the large round hay baler. John Vander Wert, who worked in engineering during the early 1970s, remembers that Dad and Arnie Mathes started working on the concept of a machine that could roll a bale of hay that weighed about a ton and was able to stay out in the field and shed moisture. It would truly be a way to bale hay or grasses with just one person.

The work started on January 6, and a prototype was in the field February 22. There were many obstacles for the baler. The biggest was getting the hay to start turning as a bale once it was inside the chamber. They thought maybe if there was something for the hay to connect to, the process to start a bale forming would work. Out in the field, they spied a fence post and decided to throw it in the chamber. Sure enough, the hay started to collect around the post and form a bale.

One of our procurement team members, Del Zuidema, recalled Dad asking him to look for cardboard tubes to use instead of fence posts. At the same time, the team was experimenting with other designs to get the bale started and was successful with a new finger design.

The baler was a landmark, a disruptive innovation that dramatically changed the way farmers baled hay. For Dad, the farmers' need had been a driving force. He often reminisced, "Boy, were they looking for a better way!" The round hay baler proved to be that better way.

In the decades since the round baler was invented, licensed, and copied, Dad enjoyed seeing pasture landscapes around the world dotted with large, round bales.

FLOW

Before starting our lean journey, Dad and I talked with Vermeer Manufacturing Director Arlie Vander Hoek about the time it took to build a baler. In the 1980s, balers were built in batches. Pieces were cut for fifty balers in the machine shop. Forklifts then moved the skids of pieces to welding, where batches of weldments were prepared. Forklifts then moved the weldments to assembly.

The assembly crew then did their best to find all the parts, hoses, and fasteners needed to build a baler properly. Some parts were painted before assembly, but often touch-up paint was needed after assembly. Since the process was done in batches, a tremendous amount of work-in-process inventory existed within the plant. It took at least six weeks from start to finish.

Dad challenged Arlie to cut that time in half by allowing one week in the machine shop, one in welding, and one in assembly.

Today, as a result of our lean journey, we have shortened the manufacturing process for many machines from raw steel to out-the-door in just a few days.

Even though Dad didn't figure out the specific process of the flow needed to accomplish his three weeks' manufacturing timeline, his challenge is exactly the challenge companies must focus on to dramatically cut their lead time to manufacture a product.

Good flow is crucial. What is one of the biggest issues in having good flow? Having the right parts. Before our lean journey started, Dad knew the importance of having the right parts at the right time. Vince Newendorp said he and Dad talked one afternoon about the parts necessary to try out a design. Dad said, "Get the designs to Bobby [Bob Vande Kamp], and I want the parts here tomorrow." If you don't have the parts, you can't build.

In 2000, I worked with a *kaizen* team in Plant 7 on the medium-size horizontal directional drill line. Ideally, a *kaizen* team includes people who usually work in that area, but also several people from other areas of that plant or another plant. The team has a charter of what they will work to accomplish during the week. They observe, identify issues team members on the line are experiencing, and begin to identify possible solutions. They implement as many of the solutions as possible during that week, then perform more observations to see if the solutions are helping solve the issues.

During the process, we were each assigned to one station. We timed each stage on a sequence of tasks. Waiting for parts was, and still is, considered waste. Multiple people on the line told me, "Just get me the parts, and I can do the build in less time than you are giving me."

More recently, I was part of a *kaizen* for the small Navigator line. We still see that flow can be improved on this line and in our other plants. Whether the painted parts need to be reworked, we fail to receive quality purchased items, or the manufactured parts have problems, flow absolutely depends on having the right quality parts at the right time.

Dad looked for better ways to do manufacturing processes, and he also he modeled several other lean principles in his work in engineering. Daryl Van Zee remembers being a bit irritated when he heard some of our lean leaders talked about the "revolutionary" new process when we started our lean journey. Since Daryl had worked with Dad in engineering, he knew that many of the lean principles were not new. They were principles Dad had often used in designing new products.

CUT THE INVENTORY

In a lean enterprise, inventory is a waste. Too much inventory creates the need to move it, obsolete it, or refresh it… spend a lot of money to simply store it. For manufacturers, it is the worst of the eight lean wastes.

I started working in the Vermeer human resources and marketing departments in the early 1980s. I had no background in manufacturing processes, but even then I often heard Dad say he really disliked big central receiving areas.

The central receiving areas held purchased parts that would be needed for assembling the finished product. At one point in our history, we used one entire 200,000 square foot plant to receive purchased parts. From experience, Dad knew that items are often purchased in large quantities to get a lower price. But then an engineering change might happen or the demand might fall and cause inventory to become obsolete. This is a big waste! So one of the things Dad liked most about lean was the emphasis on reducing the amount of inventory and relocating inventory receiving areas to each plant. In the first years of lean, we reduced work-in-process inventory by 50 percent. Central receiving inventory was also reduced. Freeing up inventory freed up cash. To a private company, cash is key for future success!

While he was pleased about reducing inventory, Dad was not always enthusiastic about computers and technology. But if he could see how they helped the company reduce costs, he saw their benefit. Dick Barnard started our computer initiative in the late 1970s. We started with a mainframe in a room about the size of a closet. Dad asked Dick, "Is it making us any money? Are we able to do these jobs and not hire as many people?"

Dick was pleased to show Dad how to use the computer system to track a bill of material for a machine and produce a list of required parts. Dad could see benefit of this process. When our central receiving department was put on the computer, Dick showed Dad that they could better track exactly what was needed in central receiving. As a result, they were able to take $5 million out of the central receiving total budget. Dad was impressed with that!

Whole goods inventory was another concern of Dad's. Jim Braafhart started at Vermeer during the early baler years in the 1970s. He worked in the accounting area for the forage part of the business. He said Dad was adamant about inventory. Those first years of the baler were intense, with most office team members starting at 6:30 a.m. and working past 5:00 p.m. Dad was concerned about the number of balers on the yard. Each Friday afternoon or Saturday morning, Jim went to the yard to count balers. He made sure he had the correct number because he knew that early Monday morning, Dad would ask, "How many balers are on the yard?" He wanted exact numbers for each model. Jim knew he needed to be able to prove his numbers, so he counted and tabulated each model quantity with great care.

My parents lived just across the road from the company, so Dad drove the roads behind and in front of the plants daily. From 1990 through 2008, Dad would often ask, "Why do we have those big machines sitting on the yard instead of shipping them out?"

Several times he asked me about the big grinders or trenchers that were sitting on our yard and tying up cash. "Why did we build them if we didn't have orders?" he would ask.

Like Jim, I knew I had better be prepared with answers before he came and asked the question! In fact, I learned that it was actually better to get the answers, then go and provide him with the information before he asked. I often went to my parents' home for lunch, prepared with the answers to questions I expected Dad to ask.

IT'S ALWAYS SOMETHING

Life is full of twists and turns. When things seem to be going well in a business segment, we encounter a major supply issue—a recall of items that stops a production line for a product in high demand. When we are close to a deal with a customer using EXIM (Export Import Bank) financing, we learn the customer or the bank needs more information or more detail. In response to these bends in the road, Dad often said, "It's always something." He was right.

Both drought and too much rain can make the forage business unpredictable. Even today, a forage territory manager will report, "Orders seemed to slow up due to what appears to be a growing dry trend." And later in the same report—but for a different part of the country—we will read, "The rain has been almost unending here. Standing water is really slowing down sales and putting crop behind." Adapting to the changes in weather that influence our sales is one form of handling abnormalities.

On our lean journey, we have learned that handling abnormalities is a key job of a manager. Abnormalities include really any deviation from the standard. For instance, when the wrong parts come in for a machine, a manager often needs to work with the procurement group to get those parts reworked or reordered as quickly as possible. Great managers try to anticipate any issues that may come up and already have alternatives in mind. They also check that all team members will have exactly what they need to start each day. That will eliminate some abnormalities at the beginning of the shift. However, no matter how well we prepare, it seems as if Dad's adage, "It's always something," is still true on a daily basis.

PACING

In our lean journey, we have tried various strategies for having a paced line in assembly. One version was to have a chain-driven paced line in one of our underground division plants. The idea was to keep the sequence of movements going smoothly and stop the line if there was a problem. Due to issues with the chain system itself, we abandoned that idea. Our chain-driven paced line was short-lived.

We have tried digital readouts on lines to help employees pace their work. This strategy is known as takt time. Takt time is to line pacing what a metronome is to a musician. Just like keeping time to music, our plants need to pace themselves to the demand levels of our customers—which is why takt time is also known as customer-demand time. When demand for certain products increases, we work to produce more products in a day.

Today, one example of a paced line is our medium chipper line, which moves each chipper from one station to the next every takt time. Takt time is often around sixty minutes, so every sixty minutes each chipper moves to the next station. A horn sounds to indicate when it's time to move. This same takt time is used in the weld areas. As is the case in many areas of our lean journey, we do not think we have the final solution. We are continually improving and continually looking for better processes.

We have also used pacing quite successfully on engineering projects. In the early 2000s, while we were struggling through the dot-com bust, we were looking at how we could expand our recycling equipment line. Dad, my brother Bob, and Vince Newendorp made a visit to a company that made a horizontal grinder and were looking for a buyer. That trip helped us decide we didn't want to buy that particular company, but we did want to design and manufacture horizontal grinders. We had designed and been selling a tub grinder for over a decade. A horizontal design would allow us to better serve our customers. We realized we needed to put a key focus on this new product idea and do it quickly.

We established a team we called "Cheetah," a term coined by *Harvard Business Review* for teams that are mobilized quickly to solve an unexpected problem that could delay a project.[2] Mike Byram, one of our track engineers at the time, was asked to lead a totally dedicated team to bring out four models of horizontal grinders in less than a year. A team of twenty-six individuals was formed from across the company, including people who were set to start working on various aspects of design, jigs and fixtures, and manufacturing processes and sales. The entire Cheetah team was no longer responsible for any previous projects; they were totally dedicated to these new grinders. The plan was to use as much of the design expertise already in present Vermeer products as possible—undercarriage systems, the grinding technology of the duplex drum, engines, etc.

Mike established a great pacing system to keep the team on track. They had start-up meetings daily. We had a regular morning start-up meeting with the entire team to discuss accomplishments of the prior day and plans for the current day. We also had impromptu meetings on a regular basis when issues would come up in order to quickly make a decision to keep the project going. These meetings proved to be essential to keep the projects moving and connect the team to the project's success. It gave the team an opportunity to visualize issues and address barriers. The first prototype was ready in six weeks, and the first production machine in six months. This first unit was the HG525 (Horizontal Grinder). It was followed by a track version of the HG525 and two smaller horsepower units, the HG365 and HG365TX. Focus worked. Today, our horizontal and tub grinder lines are the center of our recycling product line.

The principle of pacing had been part of Dad's earlier mode of management. He would check on projects twice a day before we studied lean pacing techniques. For example, when Vince Newendorp was given the opportunity to lead the forage engineering team, Dad told him, "I need you here at 6:30 a.m. and noon to talk about what we want to accomplish." Vince knew that for Dad 6:30 meant 6:20 a.m. Those conversations were no more than fifteen minutes. Dad was direct. He tended to tell more than ask. But if Vince had a question, Dad was happy to clarify points. There were times when Dad came back and what he saw was not what he wanted. Then his sound level got a little louder.

GET IT DONE

Lean is also about trying things and getting them done quickly in order to test a new process. Through our lean journey, there have been times when we did a one-day intense focus on an issue instead of a week-long *kaizen*. Today, we call that intense focus a "sprint." Just like a track and field sprint in which you run at full speed over a short distance, a business sprint means intense focus to solve an issue over a short period of time.

Dad loved this kind of intense focus. He stopped at the engineering and maintenance departments of Vermeer on a regular basis. He often asked them to do tasks for his farming operation, and he usually wanted a quick turn-around. One afternoon when he was frustrated that his combine tires were running on top of the corn rows, he stopped at the engineering and maintenance departments and wanted extensions made for the axles. Steve Haverly said, "From that afternoon until the next morning, we had an all-out sprint to get the axle extension tubes and drive shafts made."

At 8:00 a.m., Dad drove away with the extensions in place. From the cab of the combine, with a smile on his face, he said, "Isn't this company great?"

He appreciated the intense focus that made it possible to get things done. And there were many times when, as the majority owner of the company, he had no problem asking for one hundred percent focus on a certain project.

THE PROCESS WORKS

Dad was in his eighties during the 2001–2003 dot-com downturn. Our sales decreased by 60 percent in those three years. For the first time, we had to make reductions in our workforce. These reductions were extremely difficult for all of us as owners and managers.

Dad became worried that we might lose the company. So we used weekly meetings to go over what we were doing to reduce inventory in our dealerships and at Vermeer Corporation. Using one of the conference rooms, we put up charts, graphs, and handwritten papers to track reduction in inventory on our campus and at the dealerships, as well as payments from our dealerships. We shared this information with our employees. They knew old inventory sitting on our yard and dealers' yards meant we didn't have orders to build new machines, so selling inventory was a primary focus. Meeting on a regular basis and seeing the progress helped Dad—and all of us—get through that difficult time. It also taught everyone in the company the importance of watching key metrics and taking action when certain metrics were not going the correct direction.

What is a *Kaizen* Event?

In the manufacturing world, we sometimes interchange the words *kaizen*, lean, and continuous improvement. In Japanese, *kaizen* actually means "continuous improvement" or "change for the better." Often at Vermeer Corporation and other companies using the lean methodology, *kaizen* or *kaizen* event refers to a specific work event focused on improving a process. In brief, a *kaizen* event identifies issues, develops an optimal solution, and standardizes that solution.

A *kaizen* event usually takes place in a one-week time period. A team is formed around a charter of goals it wants to achieve during the week, such as improving productivity or quality. Events can focus on manufacturing or business processes. The ideal team is composed of some people who work in an unrelated area of the business, some who work alongside the area of focus, and some who work in that area. The team members from the area of focus play a key role in managing and sustaining any changes that come from the *kaizen* event. Team size can vary from six to twelve members, depending on the scope of the event.

On Monday morning, team members are trained in *kaizen* methods. Monday afternoon and Tuesday are times of discovery. Team members observe the current process. The team meets several times during the day to compare notes on their observations and make lists of possible changes or improvements.

By Wednesday, the team is ready to focus on change. They brainstorm better ways to do the process in question and test these ideas. On Thursday, the team begins implementing the improvements they have selected. Team members also write new standard-work documents, and they may start to train others who work in that process. A list of follow-up items is determined, along with who is responsible for sustaining the plan with follow-up work. On Friday morning, the team celebrates, presenting its findings to senior leaders, plant managers, and continuous improvement managers.

For nearly twenty years, we have had Friday *kaizen* presentations. These are held at 7:30 a.m. in the Vermeer Pavilion auditorium. Teams give presentations about their *kaizen* work that week to other teams and managers. Whenever I am at Vermeer, I attend these presentations because it is very important to follow the lean processes and support and affirm the great work teams do at Vermeer to continuously improve every process. But attending these presentations is also a wonderful endorsement that the lean process works.

In our brand promise to our customers, we talk about the pillar of Smart Progress. That pillar reminds us of one of our core competencies: lean processing that relies on continuous improvement. Having this core competency doesn't mean our work is finished. It means we continue using the method of continuous improvement in every part of our business. Our customers know that this is—and has always been—part of our culture. They can be assured we will work now and in the future to improve our processes in order to bring them highest value.

Many of Dad's intuitive ideas have been proven true by the practitioners of lean processes. Step by step, as we have made the lean journey at Vermeer Corporation, I have been fascinated to learn that Dad was often right.

9 | Philanthropy

A Legacy of Creative Giving

My parents left many legacies for their descendants, but one of the most outstanding is their philanthropy.

TITHING

Huisbezoek[1] (house visitation) was a yearly tradition in our church. It was an evening when we all dressed up, sat in the living room, and answered the questions of our church pastor and an elder. The goal was to explore the spiritual health of the families in the church. To us children, it felt like an uncomfortable test, but Dad flourished in this setting.

I remember on one visit the pastor asked Dad a question about tithing. Tithing is the biblical belief that we should give back at least 10 percent of our income to the Lord and the church. I remember when the pastor asked Dad about tithing, he answered in his matter-of-fact way that of course he gave to the church from his income. It was not a question to think about; it was an absolute, a given. His direct and absolute answer made a positive impression on me and my brothers.

When I became involved full-time in the business, I heard a very interesting story from one of our long-term managers. When Vermeer was just beginning, Dad's cousin Ralph, who was a co-founder, suggested that the company needed to make a gift to the church. At the end of the business year, the company had made a profit, and Ralph believed the company should give back to the church just as the owners did individually. But, as is the case for many small startup companies, there was no cash for making a donation at the end of the year.

When he was asked about this in 2007, Dad replied, "We had a good profit and no money—we had accounts receivable and inventory, but no cash. So we went to the bank and said we wanted money for donations because we had made quite a bit." They received the loan and made a gift to the church. They paid off the loan from the following year's cash flow.

Dad hated debt, so this decision to take out a loan in order to tithe to the church is a powerful example of his strong commitment to tithing and philanthropy.

MISSION GIFTING

My parents and the other officers of the company were very creative in their giving. In the late 1950s, my parents visited the Christian Reformed Church mission field in Nigeria. They experienced the rough roads the missionaries and others needed to use to get from one mission post to another or to bring their children to the mission school in another part of the country.

Dad and Mom thought of a gift that would alleviate missionary discomfort from the road conditions: They decided to donate an airplane. In Wukari, Nigeria, they met with Ray Browneye, who managed construction at the mission. Ray said, "They had spent some days traveling there [in Nigeria] and understood the value and help an airplane could provide." Mom and Dad made a personal monetary gift to the mission board in early 1959. The mission purchased a used Cessna 170 from SIM (Sudan Interior Mission). Ray already had a pilot's license. He became the first Christian Reformed World Missions pilot and logged his first flight on March 10, 1959. The plane was used to

The original plane gifted by Gary and Matilda to the Nigerian mission field. This photo was taken by a sister organization whose plane was headed to the same destination.

transport adults and children between home and school and between mission stations. These trips also included flying very sick patients to mission hospitals. Between 1959 and 1962, the Cessna flew an average of 480

Pilot Ray Browneye with one of the Nigerian mission planes

hours per year. To put that in perspective, a private pilot who flies a lot for personal or business reasons rarely logs more than 100 hours.

In 1971, Dale and I visited Nigeria to see my brother Stan, sister-in law Margaret, and niece Christy. They were serving on the mission field in Nigeria and had not been able to attend our wedding, so Dad gave us a trip to visit them as a wedding gift. In Nigeria, Ray was our pilot. Before each flight, we paused for prayer before starting the plane. Those prayers for safety pointed to our dependence on the Lord in every minute of our lives. Ray told me, "Prayer was a regular practice, regardless of who we had as passengers. I might add that the Lord answered a lot of prayers for safety."

SUPPORTING MISSIONARIES

My parents' interest in missions didn't stop with Nigeria. In the 1950s and 1960s, the company paid for half of the salaries of two mission couples. One couple, Michael and Trudee De Berdt, were missionaries to Japan. The second couple, Peter and Eleanor Boelens, did medical missions in Korea.

The other half of the salaries was donated by the Pella churches where Dad and his brother, Harry, attended and by the church of Ralph Vermeer. These men knew the missionaries needed a church to engage with and to support them in their mission.

Through another medical missionary already working in Korea, Pete and Eleanor had become committed to providing community healthcare there. Dad's pastor, Gerald Van Oyen, knew Pete and Eleanor were committed to ministry in Korea, but he also knew

Outside our home with missionaries Trudee and Michael De Beard

Gary and Matilda with Pete and Eleanor Boelens at the DMZ line in South Korea in 1963

they needed financial support. So he connected them with Dad and Harry.

Early in 1961, Pete and Eleanor came to Pella to meet Harry, Dad, and Ralph. By the summer of 1961, the Boelens were headed to Korea. They set up multiple clinics near Seoul and on the Korean islands. During the five and a half years they spent in Korea, fifteen churches were set up near the clinics. In 1963, while the Boelens were in Korea, my parents visited them. The DMZ (Demilitarized Zone) between North and South Korea made a strong impression on them.

Dad thoroughly enjoyed seeing how tasks were accomplished in different cultures. The Boelens said Dad was especially tickled to see the pigs riding on the back of bicycles. Many items were transported by bicycles, but pigs were a bit unusual.

When these couples came to visit their sponsoring churches and updated the congregations on the ministries in Korea and Japan, they stayed at our home. Our family home was a ranch-style house, built in 1953. It was a nice enough home in the 1950s, but not exactly perfect for guests. Despite our single bathroom and lack of dining room, Mom was a great hostess for overnight guests. She served delicious, made-from-scratch meals at the kitchen table.

When Peter and Eleanor Boelens visited, I was especially interested in hearing their stories. Eleanor had been a teacher, and Pete was a pediatric physician. Both were very engaging, and they became my heroes, giving me a real appreciation for missionaries.

After several years of work in Korea, Pete realized that a pediatric residency would be very helpful, since many of his patients were children. He returned to school, and completed a pediatric residency at the University of Minnesota. He also received a master's degree in public health.

Due to some mission board changes, it was decided that Pete and Eleanor would stay in ministry in the United States instead of returning to Korea. They searched for an economically poor county in the United States where health-care services were needed. They decided to start a medical ministry in Cary, Mississippi. It was just a forty-five minute drive from Vicksburg, Mississippi. Proximity to Vicksburg was important because Pete knew he would need a hospital to admit patients, and Vicksburg had a charity hospital. The ministry was established under an already-existing not-for-profit, the Luke Society.

My parents' focus on missions had a lasting influence on their children and grandchildren. In Pete Boelens, Dad aligned some of his personal mission focus with an entrepreneurial doctor. Pete in turn was able to identify entrepreneurial doctors around the globe who were able to set up self-sustaining clinics to serve people.

Later, Dale and I made connections with both the Cary clinic and those entrepreneurial doctors. In 1976, when Dale was a fourth-year medical student, we lived in Vicksburg. Dale did a pediatric rotation for a month at the Vicksburg hospital. Each day of that month, Dale rode with Pete to Cary. I spent several days a week tutoring a young woman from the Cary area. The local daily newspaper featured a column from the Daughters of the Confederacy about events in, what the paper called, the "War of Independence." It was an interesting cross-cultural experience for two Yankees!

Pete had a real knack for identifying international Christian doctors with an entrepreneurial spirit and a faith commitment. He helped them serve the medically underserved in their countries. Pete and Eleanor had learned from their Korea experience the importance of local healthcare providers in international locations. They also knew these healthcare providers needed to be given the authority to make decisions in each local area. This awareness formed the bedrock of the Luke Society Partnership program.

Pete often found international Christian physicians through Christian medical association meetings. Then he connected these physicians with an American physician and an American business person who would support their ministry. Pete maintained, "Usually, physicians are not the best business people." He had been mentored by business people throughout his career in ministry and realized the benefit of a combination of medical and business expertise.

The goal was for the American partners to support these physicians with finances, business know-how, and medical advice for their local ministry.

When Pete met Pal Oroszi from western Ukraine, he knew Pal would be a great leader of a clinic in the Transcarpathia region. Pete had been in touch with us for several years about becoming a partnership team for a clinic somewhere, and he thought the chemistry between us and Pal and his wife, Jolika, would be good. Pal and Jolika Oroszi were Hungarian Calvinists whose families had been trapped in Ukraine when the borders changed during and after World War II. Pal brought in two other dedicated doctors, Laszlo and Irina, as part of the team.

Economically, the Transcarpathia region was very depressed, with an eighty percent unemployment rate. The medical care was provided by a government hospital with no heat and no medicines. Its instruments and facilities were outdated. After making the trip to Munkacs in the Transcarpathia region of Ukraine in early 1998, we decided to become partners with the wonderful doctors there, with Dale as the physician and me as the business person. In addition to our personal donations, the Vermeer Charitable Foundation—which Dad and Mom were trustees of—helped with the seed funding.

We worked with them to get access to a building across from the local Hungarian Reformed Church. We prayed about getting this building for months. When we were finally able to get access it, the building needed to be gutted and totally rebuilt with new electric and water systems. We discovered that our lead doctor, Pal, was also very adept at construction management.

Dale had told Pal early on that our clinic needed to have light and heat and to be clean—none of which were found in the government hospital! The entire project cost $5,000. We were blessed to see the clinic open, welcome patients, add a satellite clinic, and become a center that served a large portion of the Transcarpathia region, including many government officials.

The goal for the Transcarpathian clinic was to become self-sustaining within five years. As in all international Luke Society clinics, patients were asked to pay something for their care. If care and medications were given at no cost, patients did not value them. However, if patients paid even a small amount, they did value that care. Through the years we served as partners to the Transcarpathia clinic, Dale helped Pal and the team set up a fee schedule and helped design the clinic process flow. Fees ranged from $0.25 for a blood test to $4.50 for a colonoscopy.

We met with the team annually. Some of the annual meetings focused on policy deployment and developing a set of strategic initiatives. Between personal visits, we communicated via email. The Ukrainian doctors used the strategic plans and implemented the initiatives developed by the team as well as any group we had ever worked with. At the ten-year anniversary of the clinic, we could celebrate that there had been one million individual visits, the clinic was self-sustaining, and it continued to serve the citizens in the area.

Because of my parents' example and their relationship with Pete and Eleanor Boelens, Dale and I have been able to experience a special way of gifting through our work with the Luke Society. We have learned that true philanthropic giving means giving of our finances, time, and faith.

A hallway in the government-run hospital in Ukraine in 1998

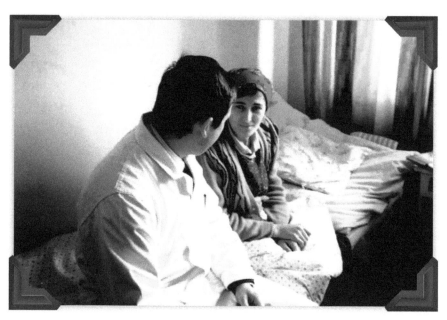

Dr. Pal Oroszi meets with a patient

Prior to establishing the clinic, doctors would dispense medicines gifted by German doctors to patients after services at the Hungarian Reformed Church.

Dale assisting Laszlo in the pharmacy

Our dear physician friends in Ukraine (left to right): Pal, Laszlo, Irina, and Ivan

The clinic in Munkacs, Urkaine, in 2010

LOCAL GIVING FOR CHRISTIAN OPPORTUNITY CENTER

Gifting money for a mission plane and sending missionaries to countries around the world were a result of my parents' out-of-the-box thinking on the subject of giving. A similar—and local—example was the 1985 trip my parents gave to multiple clients of the Christian Opportunity Center (COC), an adult residence for people with cognitive and physical disabilities in Pella. That trip transported a group of people served by COC to Disney World in Orlando, Florida. Thirty years later, some clients who were part of that trip still fondly reminisce about the special time and attention they were given at Disney.

Joyce Van Sant was one of them. She was thirty-nine years old when she went on the trip to Disney World. Joyce had previously stayed at our home several times when her mother was in the hospital. I was a high school student at the time, and I remember her as a very pleasant and appreciative house guest. Years later, Joyce noted that the trip was her first travel experience. "I never rode on a plane or slept in a hotel before," she said.

COC Executive Director Art Ruiter, also part of the trip, told a reporter, "Before the trip, the Iowa tourists studied travel skills, choosing clothing for Florida's climate, and making activity choices."[2]

Mollie Cooney of the Des Moines TV news station KCCI also went along on the trip. She broadcasted daily from Disney World and recently wrote her memories of the event in an email:

> *It truly was a trip of a lifetime for all who went. Not only had many COC clients never been on an airplane before, but many had never been out of the state of Iowa before! I remember watching their faces as they gazed in amazement at all the wonderful sights and sounds and thought...what a life-changing gift they were given, thanks to the Vermeers. It*

was very hot while we were there, but the Disney staff was so accommodating to those in wheelchairs, etc., that none of us noticed anything other than the looks of sheer delight on their faces. It has always been a highlight of my forty-plus years covering stories and a perfect example of how the kindness and generosity of one couple made a difference to so many. We were all "kids at heart" that trip!

The group from the Christian Opportunity Center poses in front of Cinderella's Castle in Disney World.

PROVIDING EXPERIENCES

Dad's generosity went beyond donating money. He enjoyed providing people with new experiences, and he loved seeing their delight. One of those gifts was providing helicopter rides for Vermeer team members.

One Saturday morning, Dad offered Steve Haverly the chance for a helicopter ride to look for deer. It was Steve's first helicopter ride, and he took it all in. He remembered Dad having a smile on his face while he asked him lots of questions. When he spotted a deer, Dad started to fly a zigzag pattern over it, swooping from a high point at the ends and low in the middle.

At one point during one of the passes, Dad stopped that motion of the helicopter, his smile disappeared, and he asked, "Does this bother you?"

Steve responded, "No, this is awesome!"

Dad's smile returned, and it seemed to Steve that the zigzag pattern got stronger.

Steve recalled the same smile on Dad's face when, during a Vermeer break, he told a story of people who had joined his deer hunting party and gotten their first deer. Dad beamed like a proud parent.

When Dad thought of activities that would benefit multiple people, he asked permission and then went ahead with the idea—and paid for it. One of those ideas was my senior class trip. We were planning to go to Chicago for a two- or three-day trip. Dad thought it would be great if we could all fly to Chicago instead of traveling by bus. He loved to fly, and he knew several students in my class had never flown in an airplane. So for our senior trip, our class of seventy students—and our sponsors—flew to Chicago in a chartered plane. One of my classmates told me recently, "The students were aware the chartered flight was made possible due to Gary's generosity, and everyone thought it was fantastic!"

1968 class trip to Chicago

Our son, Jason, spent five summers in Canada flying for his grandparents. Dad's heart arrhythmia, which he had experienced since his youth, got to the point that he could no longer pass his biannual medical exam for his pilot's license. Several young pilots become his summer pilots. But as soon as Jason got his private pilot's license at age seventeen, Dad sent him to get his seaplane rating. Jason flew to Muscatine on the Mississippi River and took his checkout ride. Then, over the summers of 1993–1997, Jason spent many weeks in Canada with his grandparents as the main pilot while Dad flew right seat.

Over the forty years that my parents spent summer weeks in Canada, they offered many seaplane rides to other guests at the camp. The summers when Jason was the "bush pilot," the owner of the camp, Jerry Lundy, walked around to ask if the guests would like a ride in Dad's plane. Jason was quite sure that most people thought Dad was going to be giving the rides, as he had for many of the previous summers. When they got into the plane and Jason got in last in the pilot seat, there were a few people who questioned a seventeen-year-old pilot. However, Jason had learned well from his grandfather and did a great job continuing the gift of airplane rides. Allowing as many guests as possible to get an airplane ride, Dad and Mom always sat in one of the benches outside and watched the plane take off and land. Dad asked Jason when he returned what he had flown over and in what order. He usually flew over the falls and another camp and trout lake. Of course, passengers always had a good look at the Lundy camp where they were guests. Dad was generous with seaplane rides, and he enjoyed seeing other guests savor the experience.

THE LEGACY

Dad believed in tithing and was a faithful giver to his church and multiple charitable organizations. However, many of my parents' gifts had a much bigger picture and impact. They made gifts to organizations for projects that would not have happened if they had only given money. They gave opportunities to missionaries, to a high school class, and to adults with disabilities. Creative gifting made Dad smile, and his creativity in giving is part of the legacy he has passed on to his family.

10 | Enhancing Community
Flourishing Through Belonging and Commitment

Early in his career, Dad wrote an article for *The Banner,* the periodical of the Christian Reformed Church. The article topic was "The Christian in Industry." In that article, Dad wrote:

> *One of the greatest contributions which a Christian in industry can make is to his community. The influence that one in industry is able to have on the local community is probably as great as or greater than in any other position. Leadership in the Chamber of Commerce, the City Council, and other community activities is an important part of a Christian life.*
>
> *I feel that many in the Christian Reformed Church have too long been satisfied with sitting back and not taking a responsible role in the activities of their local communities. Our work in our own communities must be more than criticism of local activities and leaders. It must be positive—for the improvement of our communities, states, and nation [based] on Christian principles.[1]*

Dad walked his talk. He enhanced the communities he was part of—in business, in church, and in civic life. I had the great opportunity to learn the importance of community while watching my Dad as he structured our company facilities, as he helped start up new churches, and as he engaged in projects to enhance community life in Pella.

I also have had the opportunity to help continue programs that promote care of community in the workspace and in civic life. I am grateful for the investment Dad and so many others have made into improving quality of life in work and community organizations.

TEAM SIZE

Dad had very specific standards for team size in manufacturing plants. I do not know where or how he developed these ideas, but as in other parts of his life, he created a metric for it.

Many manufacturing companies only assemble. But those that do all the machining, weld, and paint processes before assembly sometimes have separate plants for each of those functions. That structure creates a lot of travel time to connect the processes, which is considered waste in lean companies.

At Vermeer headquarters in Pella, we have seven separate plants, each with its own machining, weld, paint, and assembly operations. In the early years, this was the structure Dad thought would work best as the company grew, and it continues to work for us. During our lean journey, our consultants were very complimentary about this setup, agreeing with Dad that having all the processes to manufacture a product in one plant was effective and efficient.

At Vermeer, there have typically been 75 to 250 team members in each plant. I doubt if Dad knew the research on ideal team size, but he intuitively knew there were positive reasons to keep team size to two hundred or less in plants at Vermeer. Dad thought it was reasonable for plant managers to have no more than about two hundred people under their direction. That maximum also contributed to a sense of family and belonging. Team members could know each other by name and take pride in the work they did together.

At Vermeer, we still realize that community is important for our team members. As we have worked in teams to improve efficiencies in our plants, one particular example of community has stayed with me. Several years after we had embarked on our lean journey, I was working with Gary Coppock, one of our continuous improvement managers, to improve productivity of the D33 mid-size horizontal directional drill weld line. We started with twelve welders working on the D33 machines. After observing and getting input from team members in the area, we were able to take waste out of their processes and realign the work so six team members were freed up to join another team where their skills were needed.

However, one of the welders was quite emotional at the end of the week as we discussed the new structure. Why? She identified with the people who had been her work team. When she was asked to go to a different team, it was like leaving her family. Her reaction reminded me that work teams are a community. As managers, we need to think through team changes carefully and then explain in detail to our team members why transfers are happening.

In the early years of the business, Uncle Harry sought out people on their birthdays to give them a personal greeting. For many years, the owners sent birthday cards to each team member. I sometimes wondered whether anyone really cared about getting the card. But some people did. A team member from Plant 5 was once quite taken aback to receive a birthday card signed by Vermeer owners. He said it was the first card he had received on his birthday—ever! As the company grew, we stopped sending these cards, but we now encourage plant managers and office managers to celebrate with their team members on birthdays and anniversaries for years of service. Regardless of the form it takes, building community in the workplace is important to us.

EXPERIENCING COMMUNITY IN THE WORKPLACE

When I started working at Vermeer in 1982, I commuted from our Des Moines home to the Vermeer campus—a fifty-mile drive. When Mindi was in preschool, she often went with me to Pella and stayed at Grandma's house, which she thought was one of the best places on earth. Mindi fondly remembers that Grandma let her ride her Big Wheel inside the small house, doing a circle down the narrow hallway and through the living room to end up in the kitchen where Grandma was usually doing her work. Mindi also loved animals, and Grandma let her feed the cats that would always be right outside the garage door, waiting for the left-over scraps of food.

In 1984, when Jason and Mindi attended Des Moines Christian School, they stayed at a neighbor's house before and after school. I felt a lot of guilt about not being at home for them at the end of their school day. As I was growing up, Mom had been at home for me and my brothers before and after school. I questioned my working at Vermeer. One morning, still very conflicted about whether I should be working at Vermeer, I asked for clear direction from God. I asked God to let me know if I should keep working at Vermeer or if I should quit and be a stay-at-home mom.

When I arrived at work that grey and rainy morning, I was greeted with terrible news. One of our weld team members, Sam Spratt, Jr., had been injured that morning in a freak weld accident. He had died an hour after arriving at the hospital. We had never had a fatality in our plants, and this was devastating for everyone. One of my questions to God was, "What are you telling me?"

My first thought was that I was supposed to quit working at the company.

Throughout that day, my oldest brother, Stan, who was president at the time, talked about what we needed to do for Sam's family. Stan and I went to Sam's home and met with his wife, Patty, and his brother. We gave our condolences and prayed with them. We had decided we would set up trust funds for Sam's two children that could be used for college education or for their benefit when they reached the age of eighteen. The team members at Vermeer also donated funds for Patty and for her children

Stan, whose wife, Margaret, had died a few years earlier, knew how difficult it would be for Patty in the weeks and months that followed Sam's death. Stan said, "During the first days after a death, there are usually lots of people around to give support and comfort, but months later that support disappears." He suggested that we develop a program to have Sam's team members spend time with Patty and her children, Bill and Wendy, once a week for six months. The company would provide the funds for pizza, a movie for the family, bowling, or other activities. Team members would give their time.

We carried out this plan, and it made a profound impact on me. I realized that being part of ownership in a private company like Vermeer gave us a special opportunity to really be a community, to be a family for our team members. After that tragedy, I realized that being part of creating a caring community at Vermeer was exactly where I was called to serve.

ONGOING GENEROSITY

Over the years, Dad was supportive of providing team members with opportunities to give back to their communities by offering their time and work skills. He said, "Often individuals want to give to others or contribute to causes, but may not know how to get started. If we help organize some of these efforts, we allow our employees to feel more comfortable in participating."

Today, we still see much generosity among our team members. Over the last decade, we have had a Vermeer Cares opportunity for employees to give paid-time-off money or paycheck withdrawals to other team members who are going through difficult times in their lives.

We have sent teams of people to help with hurricane, tornado, or flooding disasters across the country. Our team members took time off to help with these projects, and often other team members donated paid-time-off money so these employees would receive pay while they were working on a disaster recovery project. Over the last ten years, an average of $15,000 per year and an average of 1,700 paid-time-off hours per year have been given by team members.

We have also implemented many corporate programs for our team members to assist them during tough times. We have offered lunch-and-learn sessions with psychologists, as well as and the Employee-Assistance Program, Workplace and Family Life Services (WFLS). WFLS is a call-line answered by a psychologist who listens and then directs team members to appropriate counseling or help centers.

The most influential program, however, has been our Chaplain Program, which my brother, Bob, was very instrumental in launching. Founded in 2005 with one chaplain, there are now three full-time chaplains who walk alongside our team members through challenges in their marriages, parenting, finances, careers, and much more. The three chaplains connect with approximately 1,000 team members every month. They have conducted marriage ceremonies, provided counseling, made hospital visits, and spoken at funerals. But mostly they have made themselves available. The Chaplain Program has become one of the most important benefits we provide for our team.

CHURCH SIZE

Dad was part of starting two new churches in Pella: Calvary and Faith Christian Reformed Churches. In each case, he was part of a group of leaders who believed that when a church grew to a certain size, it was time to start a new one. When First Christian Reformed Church had about two hundred families, he helped launch Calvary. When Calvary reached that size, he helped found Faith.

An online history of Calvary CRC it says:

> *In 1966, eleven years after the formation of Calvary, the congregation had grown to number 865 members. The seating in the balcony and the auditorium had become crowded, so families were alphabetically assigned to sit on folding chairs in the Fellowship Hall. The congregation was surveyed, and 82 percent of the returns favored the formation of a fourth Christian Reformed Church in Pella. Reverend Pontier [who was known as Pastor Art] supported the formation of a new church, and Calvary became the mother church of Faith Christian Reformed Church.[2]*

When I was in junior high, we took our turn on the hard folding chairs of Calvary's Fellowship Hall because we didn't all fit in the benches. I attended Sunday school in a curtained-off area of that same Fellowship Hall.

I was in high school when Faith CRC started. It felt like an adventure! By the time the new Faith sanctuary was constructed, I was already attending Calvin College. However, Dad's excitement about the new church probably rubbed off on me. When I was home for summers, I played organ for services at Faith and even served as its first choir director.

Dad's thoughts about the relationship between size and a sense of community influenced both the size of manufacturing plants at Vermeer and his involvement in founding new churches in Pella.

AVOIDING GOSSIP

In a small town in rural Iowa, gossip is part of the fabric of the community. But Dad was different. He was never a person to engage in speculative discussion of the lives of other people. I never heard him pass on any kind of gossip. In fact, I remember the opposite. When there were rumors about people in the community, especially people who Dad knew and admired, he absolutely refused to believe the rumor. He halted all such talk when he was part of a conversation.

He did not appreciate hearing criticism of other people either. My brother, Bob, reminded me recently of a time Dad asked the two of us to meet him at the camp. Dad rebuked us for some criticism we had voiced about one of his friends. He said to us, "You do not have the right to criticize." Throughout his life, Dad modeled respecting others by refusing to engage in gossip or criticism—and with that behavior he quietly promoted community.

CLOSE-KNIT COMMUNITY OF FRIENDS

Small groups are very common today in churches and other social organizations. However, in the 1960s they were not the norm. Nonetheless, my parents were part of a group of couples who met monthly, usually on a Sunday night after church, for coffee time and discussion. Those couples met each month for more than thirty years. One of the group's members, Harriet Zylstra, talked to me fondly of the great fellowship. Harriet said that the first study they did was on the book of James in the Bible. Whoever was hosting the meeting also led the discussion. "But not much leading was needed because everyone joined the discussion," she said.

The discussions were often lively. In fact, Dad was known to play the devil's advocate just to spark an interesting discussion. Mom was not as comfortable pushing the discussion into areas she didn't agree with. She sometimes chided, "Gary, you don't really believe that!"

Dad was a lifelong member of the Christian Reformed Church and served in leadership positions in his local church and at the denominational level. But he didn't uncritically accept all the beliefs he had been taught since childhood. Jason recalls talking about denominations with his grandpa while traveling. Jason asked him if he thought the Christian Reformed denomination had the right perspective on issues.

Dad's reply was, "It is as good as any, not much better."

And I believe that is exactly what he thought. He appreciated his heritage, but he also appreciated people from different backgrounds and different perspectives.

In addition to monthly discussions, the couples group had joint family picnics, and several of them traveled together. My parents took international trips with both Art and Hilly Rus and Bob and Harriet Zylstra. Dad enjoyed going on extensive train rides during those trips—one across Australia and one through South Africa. Dad often mentioned how he enjoyed seeing the wildlife in the outback of Australia from the window of the cross-continental train.

Gary and Matilda on a train trip across Australia

Dale and I have followed our parents' small group model. Members of my parents' small group all came from the same church. For Dale and me, moving from one church to a sister church was the impetus to start the small group. We wanted to stay connected to our great friends from both churches. We have a group that has been together over twenty-five years.

Monthly we have dinner together and a discussion. We have discussed books, movies, articles, and current events. Like the group my parents were in, we may sometimes have a leader, but there is never a problem with good participation and discussion. Our group has also traveled together, shared joys and sorrows, and just been there for each other. For us, this is truly community at its best.

FUNDRAISING FOR COMMUNITY PROJECTS

Dad enjoyed fundraising for community projects. Before 1958, Pella had no hospital. Because Dad thought Pella needed its own healthcare system, he worked on two fundraising campaigns for the Pella Hospital. In 1958, the first campaign featured a large thermometer graphic on the exterior corner of Marion County Bank that indicated the current amount of donated funds. Every Saturday night the Pella firetruck made a trip around the town square. Then someone got out of the firetruck, climbed its ladder, and painted the updated dollar figure on the thermometer. The goal for that first campaign was $450,000.

Max Hoeksema, Stu Kuyper, and Martha Lautenbach served on the fundraising steering committee with Dad. Stu Kuyper was the president of Pella Corporation and son of its founder, Pete Kuyper. Max was a successful John Deere implement dealer who knew which farmers had money. The four of them targeted people who they thought should make gifts to the hospital building fund, asking many of them to make gifts of $3,000. For some of these donors, Dad offered reciprocal gifts to a charity they liked in order to get their support for the hospital campaign. The fundraiser was so successful that they raised more than $600,000 for the hospital—exceeding their target by $150,000.

In 1977, the Pella Hospital needed to update its service facilities and expand its acute care and surgical wings. The estimated cost of the project was $3 million. The steering committee for this drive consisted of Howard Knutson, Bill Peters, Ernie Engbers, and Dad. Dad got even more creative in promoting this fundraiser. After getting permission from the Pella City Council, he had a special landing platform constructed atop the Tulip Toren, a tall set of twin towers in Pella's Central Park. A pair of giant thermometers was erected as well, one on each tower. The platform allowed a helicopter to make a landing on the top of the towers and lower a person to update the thermometers below. The thermometer on the west column represented pledges totaling $1.5 million from twenty-five Pella donors who were challenging the rest of the community to match that amount. The thermometer on the east column represented pledges from the rest of the community.

Gary landing on top of the Tulip Toren

Gary watching as Bob Nikkel begins his descent to the fundraiser thermometer

Bob updating the hospital fundraiser thermometer

Gary receiving a plaque for his work on the hospital fundraiser.
Photo from The Pella Chronicle, *August 31, 1977.*

For four weeks, hundreds of Pella residents gathered to watch the landings each Thursday evening. Dad was usually the pilot, but Larry Hutchinson, a Vermeer pilot who had flown army helicopters in Vietnam, also made some of the landings. After the helicopter landed on the platform, Bob Nikkel, a member of the Vermeer maintenance team, placed himself in a specially made seat and was lowered down the tower to update the thermometer on the east column. One Thursday evening, Tulip Queen Kathy Thies was lowered to make the update. The names of donors who had contributed to the challenge were also added on that thermometer.

At the end of the four weeks, the goal was met and there was a victory celebration. It was a rainy Thursday evening, but thousands of spectators came out with their rain gear and umbrellas. Dad was presented with a plaque for Vermeer's hard work on the drive. In a short acceptance speech, he said:

> *About three months ago, I was contacted by the board of the hospital to conduct a fund drive to raise $3 million for a hospital expansion. At that time I felt it would be impossible to raise that much money from this size community. So today I am just as surprised as you are that this drive went over the top. Quite frankly we underestimated the generosity of the people of this community. The reason this drive was successful is because of the generosity of the people and the overwhelming support that we had for this project.[3]*

Achieving the $3 million campaign goal was indeed an accomplishment. Dad knew fundraising projects like this need a focused and committed group of leaders—and also quite a bit of creativity. The helicopter landing on the Tulip Toren was definitely a step up from a firetruck ladder against the corner of the bank! And the campaign team was not shy about sharing the information about exactly who was contributing to the fundraiser. Those names on the thermometer appealed to donors' competitive spirits.

Early in their respective leadership in their companies, Dad and Stu Kuyper discussed how to fund community projects. They had agreed that the two of them and their companies would fund half of a project and then challenge the rest of the community to match that funding. They used this matching funds motivation not only for the hospital campaigns, but for several projects for the Pella Historical Society.

Dad's fundraising process has influenced all of his descendants. In the last few years, we have had several campaigns to help expand or build new facilities for the Christian schools in Pella. In 2005, my brother, Bob, and sister-in-law, Lois, became co-chairs of a campaign to build a new Christian high school in Pella at a cost of $19 million. Several times that challenge appeared impossible. While sitting in Vermeer Charitable Foundation meetings with the other trustees, Dad continued to say, "The community must be involved."

Dad had some very specific advice to the committee in the Pella Christian High School campaign:

Establish the scope of the project firmly before you officially begin fundraising. Do not raise the price tag partway through the process. Keep the campaign going within a limited time-frame. Do not allow it to go on and on. Stay on task and go after it. The match will happen only if the goal is achieved.

We devised various match programs. The first ones were a 2:1 match. However, in order to get the last push, our foundation challenged the steering committee to find donors who were new to the campaign. In addition, for every dollar raised by new donors the foundation would add another dollar. This was after the foundation and all the trustees had already been extremely generous. The goal was reached and the new campus is a fantastic facility, serving multiple communities with outstanding Christian high school education.

In other not-for-profit organizations Dale and I are part of, we continue to urge the entities to get a donor to give an initial gift that can be used as a challenge. Putting timelines on these challenge gifts provides those asking for funds with a sense of urgency.

INVESTING IN THE QUALITY OF COMMUNITY LIFE

Dad was also willing to invest in businesses that added to the quality of life in Pella, including places where families could spend time together. When I was in elementary school, we often traveled fifteen miles to Knoxville on Saturday evenings to eat at Maple Buffet, the first buffet I remember. We loved its variety of main dishes and appealing assortment of pies. During these same years, we often roller-skated in Newton, which is twenty-seven miles away. Pella didn't have a roller rink, but many Pella youth groups, church groups, and Vermeer company groups had skating parties in Newton. Dad and Mom both had learned to skate, and our family went skating in Newton once a month. The grand march was one of Dad's favorite skates. He also enjoyed skating with Mom in the moonlight skate.

Dad decided Pella needed both a good buffet and a roller rink. He gathered a group of other Pella citizens, and they formed a corporation to build the Dutch Buffet and Roller Rink.

It was located two miles east of Pella on Highway 163. In 1964, when the Dutch Buffet opened, Lois De Jong and I became some if its high school student waitresses. Saturday night was the best night for tips; many times we received a 50-cent tip per couple. I enjoyed working with Lois, and later told my brother Bob that he should ask her out on a date. I am so pleased he followed up on that recommendation and that today she is my sister-in-law!

In 1964, the price of the buffet was $2 per person. Pie cost extra. The original pie baker was my Aunt Gertrude Van Gorp Meinders. She had always been a great pie baker and was asked to take on the job. She made a wide range of pies, but her Dutch Silk Chocolate was my favorite. It had a wonderful meringue crust, a delicious chocolate filling, and lots of whipped cream topping sprinkled with chocolate slivers.

The Dutch buffet was also open for lunch. Many of our original dealers remarked that it was the only restaurant they were ever taken to for lunch, and not all of them were fond of the Dutch red cabbage that was a buffet-line staple.

We celebrated my parents' twenty-fifth wedding anniversary at the Dutch Buffet with a nice meal and program. Since I played piano and all of us sang, Stan, Bob, and I were pretty much the program. It included favorite family songs and hymns, along with songs from a new movie that Dad loved, *The Sound of Music.*

On May 29, 1971, the Dutch Buffet was the location for my and Dale's wedding reception. At that time, wedding receptions were almost always in the church basement or fellowship hall. For our wedding, Dad thought it would be great to have a buffet lunch afterwards. Having been a waitress at the buffet in its opening year, and having eaten there several times a year throughout high school and college, we were delighted to have an atypical reception with a buffet meal.

Gary and Matilda's twenty-fifth anniversary celebration at the Dutch Buffet

Bob and I singing at the anniversary celebration

Our wedding reception at the Dutch Buffet in 1971

Dale and I greeting wedding guests

Several years after the Dutch Buffet and Roller Rink opened, a steak house and bowling alley were added to the complex. The bowling alley was very popular. Vermeer, as well as other companies in the community, had teams of people who competed on a regular basis at the bowling alley. Even Mom and Dad were on a bowling team. When Stan, Bob, and I all were married and had children, we continued to go to the bowling alley during holidays, form teams, and have a family competition. Dad always beamed, and a wide grin filled his face as he watched his children and grandchildren compete on the bowling lanes.

Another investment that added to Pella's quality of life was the movie theater. There was a group of Pella citizens who believed it was important to have a theater in Pella so the young people weren't traveling to Des Moines or New Sharon to see movies. Although in the 1950s our church's denomination did not endorse viewing movies, Dad wholeheartedly supported the construction of a theater in Pella. The theater was an independent business for some years, and then later its operation was turned over to Central College.

Neither the Dutch Buffet and Roller Rink nor the Pella Theater was a particularly profitable business for its investors. But both were investments in the community to add to the quality of life for Pella citizens.

More recently, the third generation of Pella Corporation shareholders approached Dale and me to explore our interest in a similar investment for the community. Pella lacked interesting housing developments and did not have a public golf course. After several discussions with Pete Kuyper and Charlie Farver, we decided that this would be a good investment that would benefit Pella. In the early 1990s, we invested in Bos Landen Golf Course and Bos Landen Development. We talked to Dad about this investment. He warned us that we certainly wouldn't make any money on our investment, and he was right. But it was important to all the investors to establish housing options for the team members who came to join our companies and an eighteen-hole public golf course for Pella residents and their guests.

There have been many other community projects that our parents and family members have been a part of, including building projects at Central College like the Vermeer Science Center and the remodeling of Jordan Hall. The Vermeer Mill—an authentic 135-foot-tall replica of a Netherlands city windmill from the 1850s that is located in downtown Pella—was a project envisioned by my Uncle Harry. Although initially my husband and I did not know if this was a wise project, it has turned out to be a great addition to the community.

Vermeer Mill Construction in 2002

"We're watching history in the making," was the comment by one attendee as they watched the new windmill top being lifted into place on the brick base. *The Pella Chronicle* stated that the construction was like clockwork. "A gigantic crane began lift-

The Vermeer Windmill

ing the eight-sided wooden structure off the ground at 9:30 a.m. A short time later, it was resting in its position atop the four-story brick base. Shortly before 1:00 p.m., the crane carried the cap to its perch on top of the windmill."[4] Reaching 135 feet off the ground, the Pella windmill is the tallest working windmill in the United States.

After the death of my Uncle Harry in 2006, the windmill exhibited a special message. Historically, windmills' sail positions have been used to communicate city news. After Harry's death, the *Chronicle* reported:

> *The mill sails always turn counter-clockwise. If there was a reason for celebration, such as a new baby, then the miller would signify this by stopping the sail just before it reached its highest position; this is called "coming." If there is a cause for grief, the mill is stopped in just past the highest position, called "going."*

> *The Vermeer Mill was set in the going position for two weeks to signify mourning the passing of Harry Vermeer, for whom the mill was named. The Vermeer Mill was a special project for Harry and had been a dream of his for many years before it was finally completed. Harry wanted Pella to have something to remind people for generations to come of our Dutch Heritage.*[5]

The Vermeer Mill in mourning. Photo from The Pella Chronicle, *February 9, 2006.*

In 1961, when Dad wrote in *The Banner* about the importance of community, he also revealed that he valued his role as a businessman in the community. He wrote:

Much has been written for our young people encouraging them to enter the ministry or missions…But for those who do not feel called to these professions, perhaps industry can provide a real field of Christian service. America sadly needs Christian leadership in all positions of life. We are called to be the salt of the earth. I am certain that American industry can use a lot of this salt.[6]

Dad was definitely salt for American industry—and in many other parts of his community as well. His model resonated with a memorable lecture given by Gorden Spykman in the Calvinism class I took in college. Gordon drew three circles on the chalkboard. He said, "Most of the world looks at life as separate spheres. Home, school or work, and church are separated." He then drew three overlapping circles. He went on to say that as Christians, if we believe Jesus is Lord of our lives, then He is Lord of each overlapping sphere of our lives. Our faith makes a difference in our home, school, and work lives.

This world-and-life view, modeled by Dad and reinforced throughout my life, has been a cornerstone of how I look at and live in our world. Following in his footsteps, I have been blessed, and I continue to be grateful for the life and legacy of my father.

Source Notes

Preface

1. "Children Benefit if They Know About Their Relatives, Study Finds," *Emory University*, March 3, 2010, <http://shared.web.emory.edu/emory/news/releases/2010/03/children-benefit-if-they-know-about-their-relatives-study-finds.html#.WYxxnl-GQzIV> (August 10, 2017).

1. Roots

1. Excerpt taken from a Pella National Bank Brochure published April 15, 1947. The brochure can be seen at the Pella Historical Society archives.

2. "Glass Insulators," *Collectors Weekly*, n.d., <http://www.collectorsweekly.com/tools-and-hardware/insulators> (August 10, 2017).

3. *Vermeer Family History*, 1991, pg. 7.

4. White Way Auto Company ran advertisements for their Buick, Kissel, and Oldsmobile lineups in the March 15 and 22, 1917, editions of *The Pella Chronicle*. They can be viewed on <http://http://pella.advantage-preservation.com/>.

5. "Kissel Motor Car Company," *Wikipedia*, June 24, 2017, <https://en.wikipedia.org/wiki/Kissel_Motor_Car_Company> (August 28, 2017).

6. "Rural Homes to have Electric Light Service," *The Pella Chronicle*, October 9, 1930, pg. 1.

7. Ibid.

2. Equality

1. Kevin Pollard and Paola Scommegna, "Just How Many Baby Boomers Are There?," *Population Reference Bureau*, April 2014, <http://www.prb.org/Publications/Articles/2002/JustHow-ManyBabyBoomersAreThere.aspx> (August 28, 2017).

2. J.Y. Smith and Noel Epstein, "Katherine Graham Dies at 84," *The Washington Post*, July 18, 2001, <http://www.washingtonpost.com/wp-dyn/content/article/2005/08/04/AR2005080400963.html> (August 28, 2017).

3. Russell Shorto, *Amsterdam: A History of the World's Most Liberal City*, New York: Vintage, 2014, pg. 108.

4. "These Are the Women CEOs Leading Fortune 500 Companies," *Fortune*, June 7, 2017, <http://fortune.com/2017/06/07/fortune-500-women-ceos/> (August 28, 2017).

5. "Recommendation 3. Implement and encourage initiatives to increase the female labor force participation rate," *B20 China*, 2016, pg. 29.

6. Christopher Atkinson, "Value of Technology for Girls in Emerging Markets," *LinkedIn*, September 30, 2015, <https://www.linkedin.com/pulse/value-technology-girls-emerging-markets-christopher-atkins-president> (August 20, 2017).

3. Skeptical and Curious

1. Duane A. Schmidt, *Iowa Pride*, Ames: Iowa State University Press, 1996, pp. vi–ix.

2. "Biography – In Memory of Dr. William Spoelhof," *Calvin Collge*, n.d., <https://www.calvin.edu/admin/president/spoelhof/biography/> (September 2, 2017).

3. Charles Higham, *The Civilization of Angkor*, Berkeley: University of California Press, 2004, pp. 1–2. Found via "Angkor Wat," *Wikipedia*, August 27, 2017, <https://en.wikipedia.org/wiki/Angkor_Wat> (August 28, 2017).

4. "Learning New Skills Keeps an Aging Mind Sharp," *Association for Psychological Science*, October 21, 2013, <https://www.psychologicalscience.org/news/releases/learning-new-skills-keeps-an-aging-mind-sharp.html> (August 28, 2017).

4. Heart of an Entrepreneur

1. "Builds Own Tractor Cab," *The Pella Chronicle*, April 20, 1939, pg. 2.

2. Historic Pella Trust, *Preservation Update Newsletter*, Spring 2011.

3. "Entrepreneur," *Dictionary.com*, n.d., <http://www.dictionary.com/browse/entrepreneur> (August 18, 2017).

4. Frank La Pira, "Entrepreneurial intuition, an empirical approach," *Journal of Management and Marketing Research*, Vol. 6, January 2011, pg. 2.

5. "Intuition," *Oxford University Press*, n.d., <https://en.oxforddictionaries.com/definition/intuition> (August 18, 2017).

5. Communication

1. On June 6, 1935, *The Pella Chronicle* listed Dad's name as a cast member in *The Eagle Screams*, a comedy by W. Braun. The paragraph at the end of the article notes, "Each play presented by high school pupils requires four or five weeks of hard practice. Those mentioned above should be praised for their efforts to make the play successful." The play had been written by W. Braun one year prior—in 1934.

6. Tools for Success

1. The difficulty of this labor was the reason Dad was looking for a better way to accomplish the task. This search resulted in his most iconic invention: the large round hay baler.

2. Alice Schroeder, *The Snowball: Warren Buffett and the Business of Life*, New York: Bantam, 2009, pg. 523.

7. Practical Leadership

1. For more information about Pete Kuyper and Pella Corporation, see sidebar on page 142.

2. "Management by wandering around," *Wikipedia*, July 13, 2017, <https://en.wikipedia.org/wiki/Management_by_wandering_around> (August 28, 2017).

8. Lean Processes

1. "Pella (company)," *Wikipedia*, December 24, 2016, <https://en.wikipedia.org/wiki/Pella_(company)> (August 23, 2017).

2. Mats Engwall and Charlotta Svensson, "Cheetah Teams," February 2001, <https://hbr.org/2001/02/cheetah-teams> (August 24, 2017).

9. Philanthropy

1. Dutch-to-English dictionaries translate this word as "sick calls," but in my denominational tradition it referred to home visits by church elders.

2. "Pella Group of Persons With Impairments Learns How to Take a Vacation," *The Banner*, August 12, 1985, n.p.

10. Enhancing Community

1. Gary Vermeer, "The Christian in Industry," *The Banner*, September 15, 1961, pg. 15.

2. "Calvary's History," n.d., <http://calvarypella.org/history/> (August 24, 2017).

3. "Hospital addition drive goes over $3 million goal," *The Pella Chronicle*, August 31, 1977, pg. 1.

4. "Historic day: Vermeer Windmill gets its crown," *The Pella Chronicle*, March 28, 2002, pg. 1.

5. "Windmill in Mourning," *The Pella Chronicle*, February 9, 2006, pg. 16.

6. Vermeer, "The Christian in Industry," pg. 15.